Whatever Happened

to

Randolph Scott ?

WITHDRAWN

by: C. H. Scott

Historical Assistance and Editing by William C. Cline

**Published by
Empire Publishing, Inc.
Box 717, Madison, NC 27025-0717
(910) 427-5850**

Other books published by Empire Publishing, Inc.:
    The Roy Rogers Reference-Trivia-Scrapbook Book by David Rothel
    The Gene Autry Reference-Trivia-Scrapbook Book by David Rothel
    More Cowboy Shooting Stars by John A. Rutherford and Richard B.
        Smith, III
    Allan "Rocky" Lane, Republic's Action Ace by Chuck Thornton and
        David Rothel
    Tom Mix Highlights by Andy Woytowich
    An Ambush of Ghosts by David Rothel
    Tim Holt by David Rothel
    Saddle Pals by Garv Towell and Wayne E. Keates

Future books to be published by Empire Publishing, Inc.:
    Lash LaRue, The King of the Bullwhip by Chuck Thornton and David
        Rothel
    Randolph Scott by Jefferson Brim Crow, III
    Saddle Gals by Steve Turner and Edgar M. Wyatt

Empire Publishing, Inc.
Box 717
Madison, NC 27025-0717
(910) 427-5850

Whatever Happened to Randolph Scott © 1994 by C. H. Scott

Library of Congress Catalog Number 94-061282
ISBN Number 0944019-16-1

Published and printed in The United States of America

1 2 3 4 5 6 7 8 9 10

In the footsteps of the giant
I learned to face the odds
I learned that honor and respect were the keys to life
by his words and his example
he taught me to be a man
and still in my dreams we walk down dusty streets
with six guns in our hands.

Footsteps of the Giant copyright © 1994 by Chris H. Scott

TABLE OF CONTENTS

INTRODUCTION

A number of people have asked me where I get the ideas for my books and my stories as a writer. Most of them come out of thin air. All of them except for this one, that is. This one is special so I'm going to share the way the idea came to me this time.

In the early 1970s I was driving from San Diego where I was currently living to Beverly Hills, where my parents lived. It was a beautiful day. The sun was shining so I had the top off my convertible car. Of course, with the top off, I had to turn the music up loud. As I made the transition from I-5 to I-405, I switched the radio to another station. The announcer was going on about a new Statler Brothers' song. I was tempted to change the channel since the Statler Brothers were not at that time among the people I wanted to hear musically. Rare for me and on a whim I left the dial alone. Good thing I did. The song was "Whatever Happened to Randolph Scott?". I almost drove off the road when I heard it.

Whatever happened to Randolph Scott
Ridin' the trail alone?
Whatever happened to Gene and Tex and Roy and Rex
—the Durango Kid?
Oh, whatever happened to Randolph Scott,
His horse plain as could be?
Whatever happened to Randolph Scott
has happened to the best of me!

When I got to my parents' house, I burst through the door anxious to tell my father about the song I had heard. Since it was about him, I thought he would get a real kick out of it. It was about five o'clock in the afternoon and as was his custom my father was sitting in his chair in the living room drinking his self imposed daily glass of Coors beer. I ran up to him almost bursting. He looked up at me and smiled his wry, impish smile. Without a word he reached beside his chair just as I was about to tell him about the song. I hadn't even gotten the first few words out when he handed me the Statler Brothers album which had been sitting next to his chair.

God, he always did that to me! He was very pleased with himself. He always was when I tried to get one up on him. It tickled him to take me by surprise. I suppose I've learned from him in that respect as I take the same kind of pleasure in doing to others that very thing he did to me. He thought he was cute and funny when he did those kinds of things to me. I have to admit that I got a tickle out of them as well.

I remembered this story just recently when a radio station played the same song. The vision of that story washed over me. I had been pondering for a number of months looking for a just way to treat a book about Randolph Scott, my father. Nothing I came up with seemed to feel right until I heard that song. I knew I couldn't just write a biography in the traditional sense. That style would be rather dull and uninteresting to me. I have nothing of a negative nature to say about the man so I can't write a *Mommy Dearest*, the book Christina Crawford wrote about her mother Joan. When I remembered the story, I realized the best book I could write about my father was a compilation of all the stories and trivia I remembered from my time with him.

There is a lot of dialog in the pages of this book. I've tried to make it as accurate as possible; but, unfortunately, the passage of time may have lost some of the words which were actually spoken. Be of good cheer, however, because the content and the meaning will be very clear.

The following pages are the result of those thoughts and remembrances. Let me conclude this introduction by stating that Randolph Scott was one of the finest and most decent men I have ever had the pleasure of knowing. I learned a great deal of life's lessons from him. There was great wisdom and experience in his thoughts and principles. Even though he was raised in the South, where emotions are generally kept under strict control, he was a passionate and compassionate man. He wasn't perfect; but then, few of us are. Still, there isn't a day that goes by that I don't silently thank him for the love and the education he afforded me. If I had to choose a father I think I would keep the one who raised me; and that is about the best recommendation I can offer.

Chapter 1

KEEPING UP WITH THE GIANT

The afternoon sun highlighted the red in my father's complexion as he proudly and carefully tensed the elephant ear plants which are strategically placed around the front of our house in Beverly Hills. The steel gray in his hair sparkled as the sunlight played hide and seek in the lightly wind-tickled plants. I was sitting and playing in the dirt which surrounded the plants my father was meticulously pruning. I was about five years old. I looked up at him and was in awe at the concentration and care he was giving in his manipulations of the elephant ear.

Suddenly he stood up at the sound of a man and his wife trudging through the low growing foliage which set our house off from the street. They had entirely ignored the paved driveway which was only a few feet from where they entered our property. Dad smiled politely at the couple as they approached him. "Good afternoon. Can I do something for you?" he asked.

I looked up at him in disbelief. I can't count the number of times that he used to scold me about running or walking through the plants.

The man stared at my father. His jaw was slightly slack with recognition. "Mr. Scott, my wife and I would like your autograph. Would you mind signing this for us?" He handed my father what looked like one of the maps which used to be sold all over Beverly Hills and Hollywood that show the locations of the movie stars' homes.

Dad took the map with a smile on his face and scribbled

something on the map with the pen which the man had given him. "I hope this will do." He handed the map back to the man's wife and shook the man's hand graciously. "If you wouldn't mind, would you please walk out using the driveway?"

The man looked over his shoulder at the driveway and nodded his head. "Thank you for the autograph, Mr. Scott. All the folks back home will be envious." They scurried up the driveway with their prize clutched tightly in their hands.

Dad shook his head as the man and his wife drove away. Anger flashed in his eyes as he inspected the path the couple had taken through the plants. "Tourists!" He turned and looked at me. "If you were to do that same thing to them they would be shooting at you with a shotgun."

I stared at him for a while and then I could remain quiet no longer. "You didn't get mad at them. If I did that, you'd be mad."

My father shook his head as he knelt down to me. "Son, they are a little old for me to scold. The reason I tell you not to play in the plants is so you won't do what they did. Do you understand?"

I nodded my head.

He really didn't like the discourtesy which so many people displayed when they went in search of autographs, but they were the ones who supplied him with the income to support his family. Manners dictated that he say nothing to them of his feelings about their behavior. He tolerated this sort of discourtesy for a great many years, as do many others of the famous and noteworthy. Ultimately he tried to get his name and address taken off the maps; but even though Dad's attorney was one of the finest available, he failed to have the address and name removed. I stared up at him. He was so tall and big. He seemed like a giant whose head scraped the clouds from my youthful point of view. Considering his tolerance, I guess he was a giant in other areas as well.

****

A giant! That's the way I saw him, but the world at large saw him that way too. There was and is almost nowhere you can go where at least somebody hasn't heard of Randolph Scott.

The "giant," Randolph Scott, standing on the steps of his family home. Note the portrait behind him is of him in his childhood.

He was a giant in the film industry. He stood six foot four inches tall, which made him a giant of a man by the standards of his era — even taller if you are a small child looking up at him — but it was more than just his physical presence. There was a something almost regal about the way he held himself.

(Bold print career or professional background information, and movie-goer insights and reactions, were contributed to this narrative by William C. Cline.)

Certainly he became a giant in the movie industry:

George Randolph Scott was a true North Carolinian, reared in Charlotte. It was only by accident that George and Lucy Crane Scott, his parents, were in Orange County, Virginia, visiting relatives, when he was born. As soon as his mother was able to travel, they brought him home to Charlotte. He lived there with his family for the next thirty years.

In 1928 he traveled to California where he began his long career in motion pictures. He was discovered by studio president Howard Hughes, who carefully took advantage of Scott's potential as a leading man. Casting him as the male lead in such films as *Sky Bride, Supernatural, To the Last Man, Last of the Mohicans* and *Rebecca of Sunnybrook Farm*. There were also films like *Roberta, Jesse James, My Favorite Wife* and *The Spoilers*, in which he co-starred with other top movie names such as Fred Astaire, Tyrone Power, Henry Fonda, Cary Grant, Marlene Dietrich and John Wayne.

Full stardom came to him in the early 1940s. It was then that the true "Randolph Scott films" were born. Motion pictures like *The Desperados, Gung Ho, Corvette K-225,* and *Abilene Town*. From this moment forward he was more than a star. He had become a giant in all forms and by all standards.

He didn't strut. He didn't swagger. There was no conceit,

no arrogance and no feigned humility. He was proud but in a way quite unpretentious with respect to his fame and his wealth. There was no fanfare or requirement for attention when he went anywhere, but more often than not, he stood out from those around him. His presence commanded attention but didn't demand or expect it. Maybe that was part of the reason he was so well known and well liked.

In a crowd Randolph Scott's rugged complexion and warm smile attracted people to him. He was not stand-offish or aloof as many stars are. His manner was gracious and open. He welcomed those who were his fans in public in a way which few have. They didn't owe him for his presence. Rather it was he who felt the responsibility to acknowledge their contribution to his status as a celebrity. It would never have crossed his mind to squander his fame and his popularity by attaching himself to some public money-making venture like a restaurant or a line of clothing.

****

A few months ago I gave a lecture about how I write stories to the seventh and eighth grade classes at Brunswick Middle School in North Carolina. The school is relatively near my house on Oak Island, although I have driven far greater distances to speak to other schools. I firmly believe in trying to encourage young minds at every opportunity. I do this because (1) it is exceptionally flattering to my ego, and (2) our young adults and children keep me fresh in my perspective of my own writing and creative processes. Unlike many of the classes I have taught, this class wrote me letters to describe their thoughts and feelings about my lecture and my stories. The book they were currently reading was my first one, *Tales from the Tropics.*

Some of the comments and ideas I read in those letters floored me. I never realized the effect I would have on these children. It struck me that as a semi-well known celebrity, in my area at least, I have a tremendous responsibility. These young minds opened up to me as a result of my stature as a writer. To them I was like a giant in the world of adults. Aside from the fact that I am a large and imposing character, I am as well a figure larger than life in their eyes because of my occupation. In the minds of some of those children my comments and vocalized thoughts changed the way they perceived the world and their place in it. It is flattering but very frightening in its implication and scope. All of a sudden I'm important in ways which will have at least some effect on others.

I have talked to a great many people who watched my father in films, some who knew him personally and others who just saw him briefly. Is this what they saw in him? Did he, as I was doing, wonder about the effect he was having on all those people? How much thought did he put into living up to his image?

I sat back in my chair after reading the letters and the image of my father took form in my mind's eye. It suddenly hit me how much he had to endure as a star and a symbol to so many people. As a giant in a world of giants he held himself to a much higher and stricter standard. It was not just a standard which he held up to the public. It was a standard that he practiced every moment of every day. We all hold someone in our minds this way, I think. For me, it was my father, but I'm sure a great number of people saw him the way I did.

****

All of this had me thinking about my father and the way I perceived him as I grew up. Anyone who met Randolph Scott in person realized very quickly that he stood over 6' 4". He was a well-built man.— lean and well muscled. He was an imposing man in a physical sense. Add to that the square- cut jaw and the regal straight stance and you have the perception of a giant. My first memories of him are the same. He was a tall "giant" who towered over me and looked down from the clouds to see me. His well tanned face was a golden sun which shone brightly from the sky, especially when he smiled.

I remember when I was only about five or six years old my father took me to a baseball game. The Dodgers were playing a team that I do not recall at this point in time. I guess I should mention that Dad was a true blue fan of the Dodgers. He didn't wave a pennant or wear a Dodger blue jacket but come rain or shine he supported his team. In those days most of the adults who surrounded me were giants, but my dad was the tallest and most imposing of them all. When you're a child, it is amazing that sometimes you don't end up with a stiff neck from looking up at the towering adults who inhabit our world. Maybe that's why nature and evolution have allowed our bones and muscles to stay supple until we are grown. Not only are we saved neck problems but when you spend most of your time looking up, you occasionally walk or run into things that you would not have seen if you weren't looking at the "giants" around you. It was hard not to be distracted when you were surrounded by walking monoliths.

My dad hated to fight with the crowds, so he always insisted on getting to the games early. That would allow time to get something to drink and eat and also a chance to use the men's room before the bulk of the people arrived. I can't imagine that he had any trouble, but he must have thought it easier for me to navigate without the tumultuous numbers of others who would be walking around if we were to arrive later.

We got out of the car and started walking to the gate of the stadium. Dad was wearing a sports coat over a golf shirt and a neatly pressed pair of pants. If I'm not mistaken he also wore a hat which was his custom in those days. In fact he had a wonderful assortment of dress hats in his closet. It never would have occurred to him to have dressed any more casually to a game. It was the style back then to dress more formally. Not just prominent figures but everyone in general. I know that when he told me of his childhood that was one of the things he mentioned. A number of my friends' parents have told me similar stories. I guess I'm lucky that we have become a less formal society. If Dad had had his way with me, I would be a much more formal dresser now.

By the second or third step he had a reasonably substantial lead on me. I yelled from the vast distance behind, "Wait for me!" My little legs were moving as quickly as possible.

He would turn and smile, "Come on, slow poke." The smile on his face was wide and warm as he looked back at me from the clouds. His long arm arced through the sky as he motioned to me.

I watched his legs move. Each stride seemed to cover a phenomenal distance. My short little legs struggled to achieve a speed sufficient enough for me to keep his pace and cover the distance between us. The ticket gate was almost the length of a football field from the car. I was at least several paces behind my father by the time he reached the gate. I caught up to him as he handed our tickets to the smiling black-skinned man who stood by the turnstile.

The man smiled at my dad and wished him a good day by name. "Good afternoon, Mr. Scott." The man glanced back at me as I caught up with my father. He smiled down at me. "And you must be the young Mr. Scott. You better keep up with him." He smiled and winked at me.

I stared up at the man whose smile was wide and warm and shook my head.

Dad put his hand on my shoulder, winking at the man taking the tickets. "Come on. We don't want to fight the crowds." His wink puzzled me. It was an affectionate acknowledgment about me to the man who took our tickets.

I was too young at the time to have taken too much notice but what struck home in this incident was that this man knew my father! (I'll mention this a little later, but for now there is another point to be made.) He was like a giant, too, but not nearly as towering as my father. He smiled at me as I ran to catch up with my dad. He turned to me as we passed through the turnstile and asked, "Would you like a hot dog before we find our seats?" Those are magic words for a five year old going to his first baseball game. Now I don't know if the Dodger dogs at that game were any better than they are now, but in those days they were the best. I shook my head in the affirmative. The "giant" smiled at me and started to stride away. I was determined to keep up with him this time. Also there was the added incentive of the hot dogs to fire the speed of my gait.

Unlike the walk from the car, where there were almost no other people, the walk to the concession stand was like running through a forest of moving trees. I started falling behind from the very start. From that moment on I would catch sight of my father only occasionally though the tree-like legs of the other "giants". It is a good thing my father was easy to pick out of the crowd. When we finally reached the concession stand, I promised myself that I would never fall behind my father again. I stared up at the man behind the counter and at my dad. The one thing I couldn't figure about my father at baseball games was how he could put so much stuff on his hot-dog and never spill any of it. Just using catsup and mustard I managed to get it all over myself. He used to put relish, catsup, mustard and other things on his.

I also watched the other giants conversing with the other men behind the counter. I listened to their voices and watched the reactions of the other people. I liked the sound of my father's voice. It was filled with authority but there was something else within the deep baritone sounds which impressed me.

Hidden beneath the authoritative voice was the barest hint of a Southern accent. It was a humanizing tone, and there was respect and courtesy for the people to whom he spoke. Not the typical "y'alls" and other Southern idioms but the soft understated Southern warmth and the traditions of manners and friendliness that are the mainstay of the South and its history. People responded to it and to him more respectfully than to most others. Some, I'm sure, might postulate that he was treated well because he was a well-known personality. To some extent that is probably true for some people. For the great majority of people and in the great majority of situations, I think he was treated so well because of the manner in which he treated other people. Considering his wealth and station he seemed, from my perspective anyway, to appreciate others on a more basic and genuine level than others in the movie industry.

In some ways it is hard to describe. It may be the difference between speaking at people as opposed to speaking with someone. The movie industry is glamour personified and based on the reality of dreams. It is the sparkle and the dazzle we imagine when we think about the movies. Randolph Scott was a more simple man than the image might give away. He was real and he was genuine in an industry known for the plasticity of its participants. He was as thoughtful and gentle-manly on the screen as he was off the screen

As I said, from the time of that concession stand incident, I promised myself that I would always keep up with him. With age the realization of that promise has extended to many more areas of my life — not just the speed of my gait. In stature Randolph Scott was indeed a giant. So, too, was he a giant in his relationships with others around him. I've found that model of dealing with people to be one of the most valued treasures I received from him. It matters to me as well as it did to him that the way in which we relate to and accommodate others is important. The image of the Southern traditions of friendliness and manners made a difference in my father and the way he related to people.

****

To Randolph Scott integrity and honesty were paramount issues. It is another of the facets of his character which made him tower as a giant above so many others. It's not that the many others are liars or cheats; it's that to my father real integrity was one of the few characteristics of a person which could never be taken away. This laps over into his screen roles as well. Consequently, it was a great source of pride for him. It offended him that so many people were poorly founded or possessed such an alarming lack of integrity. I guess it was his Southern up-bringing; it was a throwback from another time when a gentleman or a lady was taken at their word or destroyed by their inability to live up to it.

I remember one conversation I had with my father after I had been less than honest with him. I stood in front of him with my head hung down. I must have been five or six years old.

"This wasn't the truth, was it?" He stared down at me from the clouds, it seemed, he was so tall to me at that moment. His eyes flashed a dark lightning when he was angry. He didn't yell so there was no rolling thunder, but he didn't have to yell to make his point.

I looked up at him. I stuttered out, "No, but . . . "

He sat in the chair by his desk and pulled me close in front of him. "People will judge you by your honesty. Your integrity is one of the few things no one can take from you. The truth may hurt, and it may be difficult; but it takes a real man to admit it." The strength of his convictions in his words was etched within the lines on his face.

I remember staring into his eyes. I hung my head and was ashamed that I had disappointed him.

He knew I was young, so he tried to explain more clearly. He was very patient with me when I was young to make sure I understood what he was speaking about. His huge hand gently lifted my face so that we were looking at each other. "Look at me, Son. If you lie you can't do it just once. You will have to tell new lies to cover the old ones. Sooner or later you will not be able to remember all the lies you had to tell and then you will be found out. It's wrong not to tell the truth. People will never respect you if you lie or don't keep your word. Your word and the way you keep your word is how people will judge you. Do you understand?"

I looked up at him and nodded my head. I really didn't understand, but then, I was young. It was not until I was much older that I found the wisdom of his words and acquired the ability to carry it out. I can guarantee you that he and I had that conversation many more times during the course of my childhood. He never failed to see the importance of imparting that kind of information. Although we had that conversation many times, he was never impatient, and there was always love and caring in his manner.

****

Starting with *Abilene Town* in 1946 Randolph Scott devoted the next sixteen years to making films about the American West. *Badmen's Territory, Coroner Creek, Canadian Pacific, Fighting Man of the Plains* and *Colt .45* are some prime examples. Each were highly dramatic triumphs and some veritable classics. These films were designed to highlight and portray the pioneer spirit of the Western Frontier and its hero, the man on horseback.

His films were designed to highlight and portray the pioneer spirit of the Western Frontier and its hero.

When I was nine or ten years old my father told me that he was going to take me on a trip into the mountains. It would not be just an ordinary trip, but one that would require us to ride horses a great distance into the mountains. He had promised me for several months and I remember asking him frequently about the trip. He didn't say much about the specifics of the adventure we would be sharing. It was enough to know that we were going to do it together.

I don't remember what film he was working on at the time; but according to him, he put the film on hold so that he could keep his word to me. Looking back on that event I question whether or not he truly stopped the filming of a motion picture just so he could spend two weeks in the mountains with me. At the time, however, it made me feel very special to think that his promise to me carried so much weight.

I said at the beginning of this chapter that my father was a giant. Because that vision of him stood so prominently in my mind when I was a child I used to watch him very carefully. I had to make sure that he never got too far ahead of me as he had at the ball park. We saddled the horses at the bottom of the mountain in Lone Pine along with our guide. You know when you grow up in the city you never imagine your father as being comfortable with some of the more mundane realities of going to the mountains. I knew Dad had been raised around horses, but I was raised in Beverly Hills. When you see your father throw a saddle on a horse in real life and not on the screen, it is a bit startling. He was a movie star, and he was putting a saddle on his horse. I thought someone else was supposed to do that. My father wouldn't have dreamed of anyone else doing that for him. The three of us rode for more hours than I care to think about. My backside gets tender just thinking back to that trip. Even at my young age I was well used to riding horses, but I'd never been glued to the saddle for so long a time. By the end of the ride up the mountain, I had the beginning of some horrendous saddle sores.

My dad rode tall and proud in front of me as we began our trek up the mountain to the sheltered camp site which waited serenely for us. Damn he sat tall in the saddle. His back was straight and his posture could easily not have been any better if he were sitting in a straight-backed chair. Watching him I was reminded that he must ride like the cowboys did in the days long gone. The unhurried manner and the quiet respect for the trail and the horse that carried him were obvious.

The scenery was magnificent and breath-taking. The deep greens of the pines and the shadows which flickered in them as the gentle mountain breeze wafted and tickled the needles. There were no cars or distractions. The only noises were the calm rustling of the wind in the evergreens and the soft voices of the birds who called and sang to us as we traveled along an infrequently traveled trail. I hardly noticed my father and the man who rode ahead of him because I was too busy looking at the trees and the rocks and the wildlife that was abundant all along the trail and in the woods. From time to time my father tried to include me in the conversations he was having with our guide, but I was too busy taking in all the beauty which surrounded us. The motion of the saddle as it lazily gyrated atop the horse's back rubbed against me for many hours unnoticed as my eyes ran wildly over the landscape. After a few hours, however, the movement of well oiled leather began to irritate the skin of my legs. We were only an hour or so from the camp when the burning sensation caused me to turn my attention from the landscape. I looked ahead to my father who was a short distance away. I had intended to ask him if we could take a short rest to let my inflamed saddle-sores calm down a bit.

My eyes focused on the man riding a few yards in front of him. He was a grizzled-looking cowboy but even he was slumped in his saddle from the tiring duration of the ride. Slowly my sight drifted back to my dad. Even though we had been riding for several hours, he was still sitting tall and seemingly unaffected by the ride. He moved as the horse moved. I remember him turning around to check on me. His steely eyes flashed and twinkled in the sun. His famous stern jawed face broke into a warm smile as he watched me trying my best to sit as tall in the saddle as he was. "Chris, are you doing OK, Son?" I can see the look in his eyes as he watched me. They were very warm and inclusive of my efforts in the saddle. Those same eyes which were looking at me so warmly could also seem very stern and foreboding if he was angry with me. I hated those times and did my best throughout my life to avoid that.

I was going to ask him if we could stop for a short rest, but I resisted the urge. "I'm fine," I lied. My inner thighs were on fire, but I couldn't let him know that. In my own way I wanted to be like him. To do that meant that I would have to be able to stay atop my horse as he was atop his.

There was something about him that inspired me to push myself. He was no longer a giant to me in a physical sense. Still, he was a giant in the way he behaved and moved. I'd been horseback riding since I was only a few years old. At the various stables we used to visit I had watched a multitude of others struggle to find comfort seated atop the back of a horse. My father was different. He wasn't riding the horse. With every step or sideways movement he was a part of the beast that labored beneath him. It was an awe-inspiring sight to watch him. More than other people I have observed, he was at peace in the saddle. You could see it in the relaxed expression on his face. His eyes were open and sparkling, and an unconscious smile was firmly attached to his face. More than that, he was comfortable with his surroundings. It mattered little, from my perspective at least, whether it was the boardroom, the set or the mountains. As I grew older this distinction stood out more clearly as I watched my father.

We camped at a settlement that was high in the mountains and set there as a retreat for vacationers hardy enough to make the trip. The tents had been set up prior to our arrival. It was a strange camping area. The tents were set up with walls that were solid for the first few feet off the ground. It made it nicer for the people who visited the area, I guess. Since the tents were set up for us, all we had to do was unpack. That is the idea from a city child's point of view. I tied up my horse to a tree that stood just to the right of our campsite and walked into the tent where I collapsed on the cot which had been set up for us. My thighs burned, but I was also very tired.

Dad walked into the tent smiling. "You can't rest just yet, Christopher. You need to take care of your horse." He smiled warmly at me as I glared up at him. He understood that it was a long trip up the mountain, but at the same time he wanted me to be responsible for my part of the duties. The gentle firmness of his tone and his smile urged me up from the bed.

I got up and walked outside. My father helped me remove the saddle from Coyote, the horse I had been riding. Of course Dad's horse was already stripped of his saddle, blanket and reigns. With the saddles and gear put away I figured we were done. "Can I go lay down now?" I really was a city boy back then. This was too much like real work.

Dad smiled. "Not just yet, Son. We have to take the horses to that field over there and hobble them so they won't go too far away."

I looked at my father with a stranger look than before. You have to remember that I had never been up in the mountains like this, and I had never heard of hobbling a horse. I watched as he hobbled the horses with rope from the saddle bags. After that we carried our saddles to a tree that was lying on its side. The blankets were placed over the saddles to keep the moisture in the air away from the leather. I was too young to realize that he had grown up in a time and place where riding, horses and the associated chores which attended them were common place and as necessary as pumping gas into a car.

We walked back to the camp. Dad gently put his large hand on my shoulder like we were buddies as we walked back toward the tent. "Chris, would you like to catch our dinner?" His eyes sparkled as he looked down at me. I don't know why, but he always knew just the right thing to say to get my attention.

I lit up. Fish for dinner? "Sure. Where?" I looked around the area straining my eyes to see through the trees hoping to see a lake where we could fish.

He pointed at a small stream which flowed placidly close to the campsite.

I walked over to the slowly-moving water and glanced over the bottom. I was amazed at the time. There were all kinds of trout swimming in that stream. We had only fished for trout in lakes when he and I had gone fishing before. He handed me a fishing rod which the guide had set out. He sat down on a rock on the bank of the stream and motioned for me to join him. "This is how you bait the hook," he said as he shoved his hook tenderly through his bait and then turned to see if I was watching. "Once you do that put it in the stream. You can see the fish because it's very shallow here. Do it very gently and don't make any noise or you will scare away our dinner."

I did what he said and I baited my hook with these funny little round orange things. I don't recall what they were, but they sure caught a lot of fish. As my father had told me I dipped the baited hook into the water close to a fish. It hit my bait almost immediately. "I got one!" I'm sure that my face was glowing with excitement.

Dad put down his rod and walked over to me looking very proud. "Don't pull him in too fast, Chris." He showed my how to reel the fish in. Once the fish was on the bank of the stream he pulled the hook from its mouth and handed it back to me so that I could catch some more. The area in which we were fishing was raw and wild, but it was beautiful. It kind of looked like a scene from *Last of the Mohicans*, one of Dad's films.

We caught eight fish that afternoon and a few dozen more before we finished that trip. We rode great distances into the mountains over the next few days as well. He taught me how to shoot on that trip and he was very careful to explain the proper way to use a rifle and a pistol. It was a wonderful experience. Looking back I wish we had done more things like it, but I am very glad for this one.

I recall this particular vacation with unusual fondness. I think partially because it seemed like such a big deal to have traveled so far away from home to ride horses to a remote camp in the mountains. I was young and going up a mountain on a horse was a magical adventure made more fantastic because I had the opportunity to do it with my father. Well, it wasn't Europe or the Hawaiian Islands, but it didn't matter to me. Actually, those places meant little to me; it really could have been anywhere and it would have been as special because it was with my dad.

****

It took only a few films where Randolph Scott was the major character for the public and the studios to consider his movies special or a cut above other so-called "A" Westerns. His strong, forceful portrayals of the man on horseback and hero put his unique brand on a type of film that had already become established by Hollywood. No other actor before had been able to do that — with the single exception of John Wayne, who had been Randolph Scott's co-star in *The Spoilers* and *Pittsburgh*.

Have you ever walked into a crowded room and after looking around one person drew your attention? No matter how hard you try not to, you just have to pay attention to that one person. It might be his size or his clothes; or it just might be something else entirely. Regardless, my father was one of those people.

In my early teens I had the obligation of attending a certain number of parties with my parents. Dad was still making motion pictures. There is a price to pay when you are a celebrity, and parties are only one part of it. As a result, there were always some prerequisite functions one had an obligation to endure. In private he stated numerous times that he hated going to large gatherings. He said it made him feel out of place. My father was not cut from the party mold everyone seems to expect from Hollywood-types. From personal experience I can tell you that given the choice, Dad preferred small intimate groups of friends to large heavily attended parties. I suppose I'm just like him in that respect because I learned to have the same kind of feelings about large groups and parties.

I know one good reason he disliked the sulfurous din of large groups of people was his hearing. My father had, through the years of having gun shots going off close to him, suffered a significant amount of nerve damage to his ears. The damage was so severe that he needed to use hearing aids to understand other people properly. It took many years for him to finally accede to using them on a regular basis. Consequently, in the years before he used a hearing aid away from the house, he had great difficulty understanding what people said to him. Even after he began using the hearing aids, the earlier devices — besides being bulky and obvious — amplified all the noise in the immediate environment. It used to drive him nuts when he wanted to have a conversation with the family. He was always fiddling with the volume control to avoid the feedback that annoyed him no end. I'm not sure that wearing one of those hearing aids wasn't worse than going without one. Actually, he had to wear them once he got them. My mother always insisted he try to use them.

Especially when I was a teenager I noticed his knowledge of his need for wearing a hearing aid coupled with the frustration of the less than perfect technical level of the devices. Typically I would walk into my father's room to talk with him. "Hi, Dad."

There would be no immediate response if he was watching a ball game, if he was concentrating over bills or some other paperwork, or if he was reading.

"Dad! Do you have a minute?" I'd wait patiently while he finally looked up. "Would you mind if I...," I would trail off as I realized he was not wearing his hearing aid.

"Wait a minute, Chris." He would fumble in his desk for his hearing aid. He would put it in his ear and turn it on. The squeal could be heard across the room as he turned it on and adjusted the volume. "Yes Son, what do you want?" It would take him sometimes a few minutes to get the hearing aid adjusted properly.

Usually the hearing aid would squeal a few more times. You could see the frustration on his face as he did his best to understand what was being said. Most of the time if it was just the two of us I would tell him not to use the hearing aids. I preferred to speak louder and stand closer than to have him go through the aggravation which the hearing aids created. I guess that is why my family always talked louder than most others. I still find it better for myself if people speak louder and my hearing hasn't yet reached the level where I have to begin considering wearing a hearing aid. Unfortunately the time is all too rapidly approaching when I will have to go through the aggravation of getting one.

With or without the hearing aids and regardless of his hearing condition, Randy felt less comfortable with large crowds of people than he did with more intimate groups. With or without respect to the frustration and aggravation that accompanied the hearing devices, you would never have noticed his discomfort because his proud and confident bearing gave away no hint that the man might feel less than at home among the great numbers of people one might expect to find at various functions. Although his height put him above the great majority of the people, it was not what set him apart. There was something else — something in his bearing, something in his poise. It might have been his turn-of-the-century Southern charm or his manners that were so highly respected from the time when he was reared. I'm sure it was all a part of what made him unique and individual in an industry known for synthetic graces and plastic affability.

When I was fifteen or so I agreed to go to a party with my dad because my mother was unavailable to attend as the result of surgery. He wanted some company to go with him, and I was elected. At my age I was not overly pleased at the prospect of spending time among my dad's friends, but I agreed to go.

The whole way to the party Dad grumbled. Not that he didn't relish spending some time with a few of the people who would be present, but some of the others were a bit much for him. Occasionally he commented about some of the people, but he was resigned to the fact that he had to go. On the up side for me was the daughter of the man who was hosting the party. She was a good-looking girl, and I had been looking for an excuse to get better acquainted. I'm not being trite, but as I said, at my tender age I had more important matters on my mind.

"Dad, how long are we going to stay at the party?" I was hoping it wouldn't be a long time.

Dad leaned over toward me to hear me better and thought a minute about my question. "We'll stay for a while. Now I want you to comport yourself properly. I'll tell you when it's time to leave." I don't think he was looking forward to this party any more than I was, but it was his responsibility.

I don't know why he always warned me to behave when I was at that age. I had learned my manner lessons very well.

"Your mother accepted this invitation before she went into the hospital. I told her we would put in a proper appearance." He looked down his nose at me trying to better state his point by using body language and facial expression. "She expects you to be on your best behavior. Now I want you to pay your respects to our hosts before you join the other youngsters. I'm glad you wore the blue shirt. You know a man your size doesn't have to call attention to himself. Smaller men can dress that modern way to get attention, but a larger man doesn't need to do that to be noticed." Dad believed in that. I guess I failed him in that sense since I am still firmly ingrained in wearing brightly-colored Hawaiian shirts whenever the mood strikes me . . . which is almost all the time.

We arrived at the party on time as always. In fact we were significantly early considering that many of my parents' friends believed in the prestige of being fashionably late. This was a sticking point for Dad. He hated to be late. It was a discourtesy to the people who were expecting us. Actually, even more so than his being late, he hated people to be late for him. Something in the courtesy and perception of thoughtfulness, I believe, is how he always explained it to me.

"Son, it's better to be two hours early than one minute late. It is discourteous to be late. If you are late, however, for whatever reason, it is polite to call before the time you were supposed to arrive." My father made that comment more times in my recollection than I can count. He said it with pride and conviction. Anyone whom I know will tell you that it is a lesson which I took to heart. (It amazes me sometimes how much I have taken that particular lesson to heart. It drives me absolutely nuts when people are late.) He also extended that philosophy over into making sure a given job was done as and when it was promised or scheduled. It seems I have diverged a bit, so let's return to my story.

When we arrived, my father and I walked to the door where the party was being held. He straightened my collar.

I looked over at him as we waited for the door to be answered. He looked very dignified in his gray suit. As style goes he was dressed very conservatively, but he looked good. The style wasn't as important as the way he wore it. As far as I could see he could have been in his underwear, and he would have looked just as good.

I spoke my polite words to the host and the hostess, then slithered away from the bulk of the party to search out any others of my age who may also have been roped into attending. After about an hour of meandering around the party, I thought I should touch base with my father. I threaded through the people with a marginal degree of difficulty. At fifteen I was 6' 2" tall and weighed one hundred ninety pounds. I was not one of the smaller men at the gathering.

As I entered the living room, I scanned the faces for my father. I shouldn't have worried about locating him. He stood out from the others in the crowded room as well as if he'd been wearing a flashing red light on his head. He could not have been more conspicuous. The men with whom he conversed were close to his height; but I have to say he did indeed stand apart from them, so distinctly that it made me pause for a moment. For the most part all of the men, including my father, were dressed about the same way; but my father stood apart from them in a way which I still do not understand.

My mind flashed back to that first baseball game and I could again see him as I saw him on that day. Even though we were close in size at this time, he looked larger than I can ever recall seeing him. He was at best an inch or two taller than the other men but he seemed to tower above even them. His sparkling eyes and his wry Southern smile shone out from him like a lighthouse beacon. There was no arrogance in his manner. His behavior was exemplar as it seemed that he was looked up to by the men who surrounded him. He spoke softly. It looked, from my viewpoint, as if the men listened with extreme attentiveness.

In normal circumstances I might have attributed the other men's behavior to awe or deference to the fact that my father was a well-known celebrity. In this instance I don't believe that was the case. Most of the men were well known and wealthy in their own right. No, there was something different happening. I watched, scrutinizing the scene of which I was yet to be a part. In my eyes I had always considered my father to be an extremely intelligent man but it was obvious that these men, too, felt the same way. It was something that encompassed all parts of his being from his stance to his stature to the confidence of his voice

****

I'm sure most people are unaware that the great majority of money which Randolph Scott accumulated over the years was due, less to his monetary remuneration from acting, than his peerless business sense. Let's face it. For most of the years my father made films, he was in the top tax bracket in this country. For that matter for a number of years he was in the top ten money-makers in the industry. I know I don't remember much of that era; but from what I heard him say, he took home less than twenty or thirty cents out of every dollar he earned. Actors in his day didn't command the six and seven digit paychecks that seem to be so common in the motion picture industry these days. With a keen sense for business and investment, he managed to parlay the money he did take home into a very comfortable style of living for us.

There was one instance when my father was sitting at his desk and I came in to speak to him. Papers were strewn over the top of his desk. He had a short lead pencil in his hand. As I approached he looked up at me. Taking off his tortoise-shell reading glasses he said, "Son, when you're old enough to have to pay taxes I hope you aren't shouldered with the burden which Uncle Sam has seen fit to give me. It's criminal that a man should have to pay more than fifty percent of his income to the government."

I smiled. "How much do you have to pay?"

He never answered me. He just smiled and shook his head. "There was a time that the government took ninety cents of every dollar I earned." As he spoke I forgot what it was I had originally gone in to speak to him about. He was right, however.

People in the business community looked up to him, as much for his business sense, as the movie-going public did for the films he made. The roles he portrayed on the screen engendered the ideal of decency and heroics which many of us still try to emulate. I guess that made him a giant in a number of ways. I observed all of this as I grew up and well into my adult years. At times I think I took for granted the significance of my father's contributions both as a man and a screen legend. This was most true when it came to my father having been a giant and a recognizable figure around the world as he was a good man. To my way of thinking he was better than most I have ever encountered. I expect that there have been very few of his kind. It's too bad we don't have more of them now.

****

I may be jumping the gun a little by placing this section so early in the book, as I am sure to refer to it again a bit later, but I can't resist the temptation to tell this. As I have been writing this section, it crossed my mind that I am not the only one to have considered my father a giant. Other "giants" have acknowledged him as well. The Reverend Billy Graham was a close friend of my father's for as many years as I can remember. When Dad passed away Reverend Graham asked if he could say the eulogy at the service. The comment he made which struck me so deeply that day was that to him my father was "the greatest man" he had ever had the pleasure of knowing. That day was a sad experience for my family and me, but Reverend Graham brightened it, even though he drew many tears from me in doing so.

I don't recall all that Billy Graham said that day even though I have it on tape. But, I do recall the one particular sentiment he passed on to me that gray day when we returned my father to the earth of his home (I will remember the words for the rest of my life.), when Reverend Graham said that Randolph Scott was the greatest man he had ever known. I saw the truth of that in his eyes as he spoke. Through all the years when my father was alive and I was with him, I saw it in the eyes of countless others, as well. To me, as all the others, he is the greatest man I have ever known. He wasn't just a person or an actor who mouthed the words written in a script but an example of the way people should be.

His films and the roles he portrayed gave a certain heroic ideal that many from my generation and generations before have tried to emulate. I'm sure most will consider those roles just the product of some semi-famous script writer, but that isn't the way it was. For the great majority of the roles which Randolph Scott brought to the screen he was less an actor and more a man who simply portrayed himself. In those roles he symbolized the ideals of a man who, in a given situation, will do those extraordinary things which history will label as heroic or "above and beyond" — a person, man or woman, who in a given circumstance, will be both strong and compassionate at the same time. It was more than just a part. It had to do with the personal beliefs and standards of the man inside. I don't think his roles were chosen intentionally, but I think he migrated toward most of them as a function of the comfort of the message which the character passed to the audience. Certainly the characters were not real life. They were not supposed to be, but the messages the character represented were valuable.

Here is Dad with Billy Graham at the Eldorado Country Club in Palm Desert, California.

It was my father's way to always consider the right course of action to defend or come to the aid of those not blessed with the physical strength or the acute intelligence to persevere. He was a shrewd businessman, but it would never occur to him to take advantage of a situation to further himself or his point. In the face of those who might disagree with his opinions, he would stand up and be counted for the causes in which he placed his belief. He lived by and believed in his own convictions. Changes in time and political climes did not give him cause to waver from the beliefs that had been ingrained in him through his lifetime and his training. It was a matter of pride for him that a man or woman be true to his or her own personal beliefs. Time, education and experience taught him not to be rigid in his view of the world. This is not necessarily true of all people as age tends to make most of us (including me) more rigid and less changeable in our beliefs and opinions. He was more than capable of escaping the bonds of the old and the outmoded thoughts and ideologies that may have once been accepted as valid.

Not surprisingly, Randolph Scott played a Western character with a Southern background. In 1952 he starred in *Hangman's Knot* as the leader of a contingent of Confederate guerillas. In the film a band is led by Randolph Scott to rob a shipment of gold from a Union military unit and later learn that the Civil War had ended. Technically, this made the raid and the consequent theft of the gold a criminal act rather than an action of the war. The rest of the picture follows the confederate leader's efforts to make everything right.
Randolph Scott was proud of his Southern heritage. In roles such as this he was allowed the opportunity to show the world the decency and the dignity inherent in the people of the South. Of course, he was that way in his personal life as well.

My father was born in the deep South. I know that there has been at least a little bit of controversy over which city and state claim him as their native son. Randolph Scott was born in Orange, Virginia, but moved with his parents shortly afterward to Charlotte, North Carolina. To him there was no question as to which of the two cities he called home. When he passed away a number of years ago, he was laid to rest beside his father in a cemetery just to the side of the downtown section of Charlotte, North Carolina. I never heard him claim any other city in all the time I was around him.

When the civil rights agenda became a heated topic in the 1960s, I wondered if my father's upbringing in the South ever affected his view of people. It's not that I ever believed or saw any evidence that he was prejudiced towards people of color; it's just that I wondered how strongly the racial attitudes of the South shaded his perceptions of the civil rights debates that seemed so prominent in that era. I know that growing up in Beverly Hills I'd had the opportunity to hear a number of prominent personalities mouth off quite negatively about blacks and other minority groups. I never heard Randy comment about the subject and it made me wonder.

I discovered the answers to those silent questions in the late 1960s. The Los Angeles Police Department held a celebrity golf tournament. Since my father always tried to include me in some of these functions, he asked if I would like to join him as part of his foursome. They paired us with Jack Lemmon and Dale Robertson. Now I'd admired both men for many years but had never had the opportunity to meet them until this tournament. Unfortunately for Dale Robertson and me there was a football game on at the same time as the tournament. It turned out that at that time Jack Lemmon and my father were equally needful of listening to the game even though they were playing in the match.

On the fourth tee my father and I hit blazing drives down the middle of the fairway. Since we were sharing a cart he rode over to his shot where Jack and Dale waited patiently. I watched him make the shot and then turned my attention to lining up my shot. I knew that Dad would be joining me momentarily so that I could choose my club. After a few long seconds I looked back over to where my father had parked the cart to make his shot. I yelled, "Dad, could you bring the cart over so that I can get my club?!"

There was no response. He and Jack Lemmon were standing at the back of the cart. From my view point it looked like they were huddled over something at the back.

I walked over to find out what the problem was. "Dad, is there a problem with the cart?"

My father waved at me to be patient. I'd seen that wave before when I walked into his room and a ball game was on television. He would be sitting on his earth brown, over-stuffed chair, and the arm would come up at me signaling a vital play was in progress. This is exactly what was happening here. As I approached, I could hear the faint sounds of a radio broadcast announcer calling the action of a football game.

"Come on. catch it," my father was speaking to the radio. When the play was completed, my father looked over at me and smiled. "I'm sorry, Son. Was there something you wanted?"

I took a club from my bag and shook my head. "No, Dad. I just wanted to get a club." Shaking my head and chuckling as I walked, I made my way back to my ball.

My father winked at Jack Lemmon. "This is a very important game, Chris." He looked a little like an imp. His smile was cheery and his eyes twinkled like a devilish child's eyes might when he is plotting or toying with you.

I smiled at him and took my shot knowing full well that his mind was in two places. I never understood how he could do that and know exactly where he was in both things on which he was focused. God knows my father loved his football games, but the tournament was important as well. He was that way at home, too. If you wanted his attention you had to wait until there was a lull in the game unless your conversation was a part of his concentration split. Somehow I knew his behavior on that hole would continue until the game was over.

I thought we would never get through that round of golf. My father and Jack would stop the golf cart on the fairway way short of the balls if an important play was taking place in the football game. They huddled around the radio like a couple of junkies who were getting a fix. If the play went well, they would cheer and dance. Only after the play was over would they get around to hitting the ball. I was amazed that none of the golfers behind us got irritated. Maybe, they too were listening to the game; because as I said, no one seemed to get angry about the slowness of our foursome. You've got to admit it's a little bit embarrassing to watch two highly-respected actors hooping and hollering around a cheap radio while other golfers are waiting to play through. Considering my father's reputation and his affable nature there is little chance anyone would have gotten perturbed.

Eventually we finished all eighteen holes. We parted company with Jack Lemmon and Dale Robertson close to where the refreshments were being served. People milled around. They were a mixture of policemen and celebrities. Most of them I didn't know, but I recognized a great many from movies and television. We waited in line to get something to drink and a quick bite to eat.

Refreshments in hand we looked around for a place to sit and relax. There were a number of men at different tables waving at us to join them. We began to walk to one of the far tables when a pleasant looking black man who seemed to be in his late forties or early fifties looked up from his drink and smiled at my father, saying hello to him by name. Dad smiled at him and turned over his shoulder to me. He said, "We'll sit here if you don't mind."

I nodded my agreement.

For the life of me I cannot remember the man's name but he had worked on a number of films with my father. They spoke to each other as if they had been very close friends. Now, my major field of study in college was psychology, and through the years I have become very good at interpreting body language. I can still see the two of them clearly, even today, over twenty five years from the time it happened. They liked each other and recounted stories and light gossip about people they hadn't seen in a while. I just sat and listened, enjoying watching the two of them.

A few minutes later a couple of other men who were obviously friends of the first one joined us. We must have sat for the better part of an hour with them. There were no skin colors at that table. They were just a few men who had worked together enjoying each other's company on a pleasant afternoon. I liked that. There was no politics and no issues — just life and acceptance. When we left the table my father patted the man on the back and smiled. The man rose and shook his hand. The looks in both men's eyes were warm and affectionate.

The drive back to the house was not particularly long, but it held sufficient time to ask a few questions of my father. I really wanted to know at that moment what his feelings were about the equality of people and his view of their rights. What he told me pleased me. It's one of the things that always made him appear as a "giant" to me. Yes, he had had a few moments in the past when prejudice had reared its ugly head; but being a thinking and adaptable man, he saw the silliness of such attitudes and altered his perception and his way of dealing with those situations. Prejudice is such an ugly issue. It's nice to know that it doesn't involve someone you look up to.

I can best sum up my point by giving you another example. I made a comment once about a man I saw walking to the concession stand at Dodger Stadium. I must have been all of ten or eleven years old. "Dad, look at that man. He's funny looking," I said. I was old enough to have known better but foolish enough to have made the comment anyway.

My father smiled at me. It was one of those "You ought to know better than that" kinds of smiles. Also hidden in that smile was something he wasn't telling me. "It's a good idea not to judge people from the way they appear. The outside doesn't tell you very much about what kind of person they are," he replied. A wry smile creeped across his lips.

I nodded my head, but I was still pretty young and the man looked odd to me. We walked up to the concession stand and ordered a few hot dogs. The man I had seen was at the stand as well. A big smile crossed his face as he looked over at us. "Randy, how are you? I haven't seen you in a while." He stepped over to my father.

Dad smiled back at the man. "Good to see you, Jack. I'd like you to meet my son Christopher."

I held out my hand to shake his hand. "It's very nice to meet you, Sir." I was embarrassed about what I had said earlier. When we walked back to our seats I looked up at my father.

"Who was that man?" I asked sheepishly.

He smiled his all-knowing smile toward me as he always did when he made a point and he realized that I had finally gotten it. He really didn't have to say anything as the expression on his face drove the point home, but he did. "He is a friend of mine from the studios. He and I have worked on a number of films together." My father chuckled furthering my embarassment. "He doesn't like to dress up when he goes to the games."

I nodded my head. I had definitely been put off by the grubby sweat shirt and the well-worn denims the man had been wearing.

Neither my sister nor I had ever been taught to be closed-minded nor prejudiced in our view of the world and the people in it. It was somehow comforting to know that after all the years of his preaching to us about the value of not judging people by their appearances that my father was not just paying lip service to some abstract ideal. I've read and observed that as people age it becomes harder for them to change their views and opinions. It's nice to know that it doesn't necessarily have to be true. If one's reasoning and mental faculties remain sharp and are constantly refreshed by events and education, there is no way that they can become stale and rigid.

Maybe I can illustrate my point better by stating it a different way. From the time of my father's birth, the world has undergone tremendous changes. From his early childhood in North Carolina, where I understand from some of Dad's stories he used to walk or ride a horse to school. (And yes, I heard more than enough of Dad's stories about how he walked through waist-deep snow for several miles just so he could go to school. I think that is something they used to teach fathers to say so that they could motivate their children. I guess the hardship is supposed to sound impressive in its scope and the history it intrinsically carries with it, but I'm not so sure that it works. After all when you are raised in Beverly Hills you are picked up by bus or driven to school by one or the other parent. Snow is something you ski on.) He watched as the world and this nation evolved far enough to send a few people to the moon. It seems to me that his mind must have been reasonably flexible to have coped with all the vast and sometimes furious changes which occurred in that lifetime.

Not all people are lucky enough to have been that adaptable. All of us have seen them. Occasionally we hear people talking about how wonderful the good old days were and how we would be better off if they were still around. I never heard my father speak of the past that way. The past was history. It taught lessons that helped us in the present and gave us wisdom to correct mistakes already made so that we might plot our courses more intelligently. He remembered the past fondly, but he believed in making the present and the future all that it could be by the completion of our dreams and desires. Of course, this takes into account a strong and healthy respect for all those around you. Dad never believed in stepping on others to achieve a self-centered goal. Hard work and integrity were the cornerstones of his philosophy in success along with good manners, courtesy, learning, compassion and kindness.

I was in my early teens when my father took me aside to chat with me because I had taken advantage of a fellow student to get ahead in a class. He sat me down with a stern look on his face. "Son, hard work is a reward in and of itself. If you use another person to get ahead, it takes away from you inside. You may get ahead for the moment by doing it but sooner or later people will figure out what you are doing. It will catch up with you and good people won't want to be around you because you take advantage. It's just not proper."

I felt myself sink deeply into the chair as my father spoke to me. He was so imposing when he spoke about something that was wrong. I didn't like doing the wrong thing, but at the same time, there was such power and force in his speech and the way his eyes flashed when he spoke.

I alienated a number of good people in my time until I learned that particular lesson. I had a good teacher, though, and he taught by example. Too often I think parents expect us to listen to what they say and ignore the fact that they cannot live up to the ideals they espouse. That was not true in my father's case. He lived up to all the principles that he taught me. He had to, as to him they were more than just ideas and words.

****

Before I close this section off, I think it is worthwhile to express a few other thoughts which I feel have merit .

All of us have people that we use as we are growing up as examples and role-models. In our youth they are the "giants" who move through reality in a manner that is either appealing or impressive. The reasons we look up to them are as varied and diverse as we ourselves are. Money, power, status, image, control and thousands more are reasons. All of them are personal and peculiar to each individual, but there are also many commonalities as well.

For my generation, at least, we had our heroes from the movie screen. There were others who we all wanted to emulate, of course, who were not characters from the movies but were people like my father and John Wayne and Errol Flynn creating idyllic models through their roles which we wanted to emulate (This should not be offensive to women but as I grew up, my heroes and role-models were male. I'm sure that many of you derived your role-models from many of the women of that time.). When you consider some of the books that have come out about some of these actors, many of them were less than inspiring off screen. In my case that simply wasn't true. Randolph Scott was a good man. He was true to the characters he portrayed in his films. Integrity, loyalty, and doing the right thing regardless of the price were just a few of his noteworthy traits both on and off the screen. Films may not have made him a giant worthy of emulation, but his character and beliefs certainly did.

In reality, all of the characteristics and attributes that he possessed on the screen, were true of him in real life. Whether he had been an actor or just a simple business man, he would have been a giant just because of the ideals he espoused and embodied. I think that without respect to his prowess and power as a well-known celebrity, he would have been treated like the giant I grew up respecting. It could be no other way. The depth of his convictions and the power of his insight are considered a formidable set of attributes in the eyes of most people.

Chapter 2

ON THE WAY UP

As I grew up, there were two things that absolutely drove me to distraction. The first one of these was my mom's fault. She didn't do it very often, but when I was young and I had done something wrong she would say, "Wait until your father gets home." God, I hated that expression! I would spend the rest of the day in absolute terror until I heard or saw my father's car turn into the driveway. I'd wait in my room for the "punisher/ giant" to come and visit me.

Imagine the scene if you will. There I was a small child sitting on my bed expectant and frightened waiting to be punished for a crime which by that time had been forgotten. Young children are like that. The attention span is rather — shall we say — limited. Events don't last for great lengths of time in a child's thoughts. The only thing which kept repeating through my mind was the threat, "Wait until your father gets home." The closer it got to the time when my father would get home, the louder that phrase would resound in my young mind.

I could hear the car door being shut in the garage when Dad arrived at the house. Imagination at full speed, I could almost hear the ground quake as my father, the giant, walked to my room. The door to my room would open and the giant would look in at me. Thank the stars that my father wasn't into spanking. Most of the time he would talk to me about what I had done wrong, although there were a few occasions when I received a few swats from his huge hand. The real threat was his heavy leather cowboy belt. He never used it on me, but it was an intimidation that served more than once to keep me in line. Just having a giant standing over you with the air of displeasure about him was more than enough to get my attention.

My dad wasn't an overly physical man to my sister and me when it came to punishment. This is really a good thing considering his size and strength. (Oh God, now there are going to be those of you who are going to think that Randolph Scott beat his children when they misbehaved. I think not. Discipline was always tempered with understanding and the goal of allowing the children to realize what we had done wrong.) As a father he preferred non-violent punishments. He also chose to talk about the things we had done wrong. I was punished in other ways, such as loss of privileges and the like, but for the most part my father preferred to discuss transgressions. I guess he had hoped that by illustrating the point and the proper behavior, it would reduce the likelihood of it occurring again. I'm sure I drove him up the wall because it took me so long to learn the lessons. History will show that it took me many times of messing up to get things right. Patient and caring, he would reteach the lesson hoping that this time I would get it right.

The other thing that absolutely drove me wild as a child, as a teenager and as an adult was that I could never get away with anything without my father knowing about it. It was as if he had an internal sense that something untoward was going to happen. With his steely eyes he could see through my best stories and always glean the truth. When he looked into my eyes it was like he could see through them as if they were windows to my thoughts and reasoning. In looking into his eyes I could see the cogs of his mind turning. I just knew that he knew if I was not being truthful. If I fabricated a story, his eyebrows would rise, with one being a little farther up than the other. His eyes would pierce me as I spoke, and I just knew that he could see through me.

In all the time I was in junior high and in high school, I think I only "ditched" or deliberately missed classes a few times. One time was to attend the funeral of a good friend's father. I felt that it was incumbent upon me to give my friend support, but my parents didn't see things that way since I hardly knew the boy's father. Dad wouldn't give his permission to attend; so I left my school, which was in West Hollywood, and I walked back to Beverly Hills so I could be with my friend. I think my father knew I was going to do it, but he let it slide until that night. He was angry but he sat down and talked with me about it. One thing about Randolph Scott as a father: he was fair. He listened to my explanation and then grounded me for a week. No big deal. At least he listened to my reasoning. I had disobeyed and I was punished, but it was a comfortable resolution since I had nothing special planned for that week anyway. I failed to mention that to my father.

The big deal came when I was sixteen years old. It was the day I was supposed to be back in school from Easter vacation. I had every intention of going to school, but a friend of mine called me and told me that the surf was up at a beach that I used to frequent. (In those days I was a dyed-in-the-wool surfer.) My parents were supposed to be in Palm Springs for another day or more. I was supposed to be old enough and responsible enough to be depended upon to be without them for a day or so. Obviously not, as I felt relatively safe in ditching school as there would be no one home to catch me.

I drove to school and made my excuse to the dean of the school during the middle of the first period of classes. "Ordinarily, I would try to stick out my classes but I think I ought to go home, Sir. I'm really not feeling very well. . ," I lied.

The dean of students looked me over. I don't think he believed me, but since I had so rarely been absent due to illness, he let me slide. I am not a very good liar as my past will most certainly verify. "All right, Chris. You go home and I hope you feel better," he replied with sincerity in his voice.

I felt badly about lying but I felt compelled to if I wanted to take advantage of the surf, which was pounding my favorite beach and calling out to me with inaudible strains. I could feel his eyes boring into me as I walked out of his office. I did my best to try to look as badly as I could. I played the part perfectly, to my mind at least. (There were times when I was growing up that I wondered if maybe I should become an actor. I was most always believable. I thought I was believable. In later years I discovered that it wasn't believable to anyone.) Fortunately for me, the parking lot for the school was well out of sight of the administration building, so the headmaster never saw that my surfboard was in my car. Nor did he see the expanded smile on my face as I walked across the campus.

I zipped down to the beach and was in the water surfing before nine-thirty. It never crossed my mind that the headmaster of the school would call my parents and tell them that I was sent home due to illness. (I didn't find out that my father was called by the school until years later when my father and I were talking about this subject.) I surfed the day away, blissfully ignorant of the reality of being found out. My parents were, after all, more than one hundred miles away.

Not wanting the neighbors to suspect that something might be out of line, I made sure that I left the beach early enough in the afternoon so that it would appear I was just getting home from school. Some of them were just nosy enough to be checking on me because my parents were out of town. I knew the surfboard on my car would be meaningless to the neighbors because most often I had it on my car anyway. To complete the charade I wore my school uniform home from the beach to eliminate any other errant suspicions. I drove down our dead-end street blissful that I had, for a change, gotten away with the perfect ditch. Sadly, I was very mistaken.

I put my surfboard in the garage and headed to the kitchen to get a snack. Paddling and surfing for the better part of a day tends to make a growing teenager very hungry. I had a big smile on my face until I swung open the kitchen door. I was expecting to find the cook. Instead, I damn near dropped my drawers when I pushed through the door and saw my father sitting at the kitchen table. He looked up at me from the newspaper he was reading and smiled. Dad had that kind of "you aren't as smart as you think you are" smile that crossed his face when he has just accomplished something unique and something stealthy. My father's expressions were a wonder. Damn! He had smiles for all occasions, even when he was angered or perturbed.

I was busted. I was caught in that act with no way to disguise my actions or my motivations. It's too bad there were no large rocks to crawl under in our kitchen. The way I felt at that moment I would have crawled under it for the next decade.

I smiled sheepishly at him. "Hi, Dad. What are you doing here? I thought you were going to stay with Mom in the desert for a few more days." I swallowed hard as he stood up. He had taken off the jacket to his suit earlier to be comfortable while he waited for me. This was not a good sign for me as I awaited his response.

He shook his head as he stood up. He picked his jacket off the chair beside him where it had been neatly folded and put it on. "I came home early because I felt badly about your being here alone for a few days. When I opened the garage, imagine how surprised I was that your surfboard was missing."

I was waiting to hear my punishment. I just stood there with a stupid grin on my face waiting to hear what punishment he had in mind. I could barely talk. "Listen, Dad. I just wanted to say . . . ," I began.

He shook his head and smiled at me. "If you had wanted an extra vacation day you could have just asked me to make an excuse for you and I would have considered it." His eyes narrowed. He wasn't angry, just disappointed.

Now my mind would never have conceived of such a simple solution to the problem of needing an extra day. My feeling was that my father would never have gone for getting out of a day of school just because it was something I wanted to do. My God! How can you possibly know what to expect? Just when you think you have someone's style down pat, they change it on you. More aptly I just didn't understand him all that well. That's what I get for being a teenager.

I guess he had taught me too well that responsibilities were to be taken as a priority before things that you wanted to do. School certainly seemed to fall into that category. I guess I didn't want my dad to think I was a flake, that I would give up a school day for a less than lofty pursuit. I should have thought this plan out more. If I had I might well have asked my father but old habits are hard to break. It's not that I couldn't have asked him; it's just that my father intimidated me. It was not intentional mind you. It was never anything that he did. It was in my own mind. I always wanted to measure up in his eyes. It took me a great number of years to stop trying to measure myself by his yardstick.

****

During the year 1950 Randolph Scott made *The Nevadan, Colt .45 and The Cariboo Trail.* This was also the year when Randolph and Patricia Scott adopted Christopher, their first child. Adopted while only a few weeks old he was taken home and made a part of the family. Two years later the Scott's adopted their second child, Sandra. Legally and otherwise these two children have been the beloved of Randolph and Patricia Scott.

Only over time through dealings with other people and in reading the volumes of fan mail did Christopher and Sandra learn how much impact their father had on the public and how well received their father was as a function of the ideals and character he displayed on the silver screen.

I know I have more-than-over-used the term that my father was a "giant" in my eyes in a number of different ways but it was true. It's a hold over from the time when I was young and growing up. He was a tall imposing figure as were many of the people with whom he associated around the studios. He was also very confident in his manner and seemed comfortable in all situations. From time to time he took me to the studios. I don't remember much of the time I spent on the sets. There are, however, a few specific instances and things which I recall. This is when I developed the attitude that I didn't want to let my

Here is Mom and Dad the year I was adopted.

father down.

I think I was four or five years old. More than likely, I was five because I recall we drove to the studio in my father's 1955 T-Bird. At the studios there were cowboys walking around with their gun belts filled with bullets. Horses walked and galloped through the mock town and the surrounding sets, kicking up small dust storms that the occasional light breezes would whip into small twisters and dust devils. It was fascinating. I'm sure my father had a heck of a time trying to keep me with him while he attended to whatever business had brought him there. He was talking to a number of men, two of whom were dressed as cowboys. I had been told not to wander away. This was a tall difficult order considering we were standing on a western street with cameras and people and horses. The movement and the newness of the set was all quite distracting.

Five year olds are very difficult to keep still in normal situations. It was more difficult, to be sure, in a studio back lot where a picture was being filmed. Every time my interest waned, I got fidgety. My dad's large hand kept me from wandering off to follow a horse or another cowboy who might pass by. Dad was like that. He knew intuitively that a boy my age might wander off at the slightest provocation so his hand was his gentle manner of keeping tabs on me. Since there was no way I could follow my instincts, I had to content myself with available interests, not the least of which were the bullets in the gun belt of the man with whom my dad was speaking.

I don't recall how I did it, but I took one of the bullets from the man's leather gunbelt. I fingered it for a few minutes unnoticed until my father and he had finished their conversation. When we started to walk away, I shoved the lead-headed bullet into my pocket. In the car I felt the lump in my pocket and remembered the bullet. I pulled it out and inspected it very closely paying attention to the cool smoothness of the metal.

My father looked down at me when we stopped at a traffic light. He probably was noticing the extreme silence in the car which was unusual for me in those days. "What have you got there, Christopher?" Dad never failed to notice when I got quiet. It was out of character for me unless I was getting into something. He had a sense about that. His mind was too well ordered to have missed something as unusual as my being quiet.

I held the bullet up to him and smiled my winning five year old smile.

With eyes narrowed and flashing, he stared down at me and the shiny bullet I held in my adolescent hand. "Where did you get the bullet?" It was a quietly spoken question, but I think he knew the answer without asking.

Proud of my new toy I smiled up at him. "I took it from the gun belt of that man," I continued. "The one you were with."

He didn't raise his voice, but it was clear he was less pleased than I with my new acquisition. "We are going back to the studio right now, and you are going to give the bullet back." He turned the car around and started driving back to the studio.

We were almost home. I looked up at my father feeling very badly that I had disappointed him so much. "I'm sorry. He had so many. I just wanted one." I was a child; that line of logic seemed innocent enough to me, but not to my father.

My dad looked at me for a moment while at a signal light, shortly after we had turned back to the studio. "I've told you before that it isn't right to take things that don't belong to you. If someone took one of your toys you would be mad because they didn't ask you, right? You do know the difference between taking and asking permission, don't you, Son?"

I nodded my head.

"When we get to the studio you are going to take that bullet back to the man you took it from, and you are going to apologize to him for taking it." I know that some parents might have swatted a child or yelled at him or her for that kind of behavior, but that was not my father's way. If one of us did something wrong we were taught to appreciate the error of it and to act. In this case it was giving the bullet back to the man to whom it belonged.

The way he spoke to me it was obvious that I wasn't going to be able to change his mind, so I sat silently for the rest of the drive. I know he said some other things to me about the differences between right and wrong but I couldn't hear them.

I was too busy worrying about having to give the bullet back. I also was very ashamed for having disappointed my father and making him upset with me. I felt small. I had done something wrong, but more importantly, i had displeased my father. I looked up at him with tears forming in my eyes as we turned into the parking lot of the studio. "I really am sorry for taking the bullet," I sobbed.

Dad looked down at me. "I know, Christopher, but you have to learn that you cannot take things that don't belong to you." Getting out of the car he put on his sports jacket and waited for me to join him. He took my little hand in his large hand. He waved to the guard at the entrance as we walked quickly onto the set.

We walked through the dusty streets of the western town looking for the man I had to face. In my young mind I was hoping that we would not be able to find the man from whose gun belt I had taken the bullet. I wasn't going to be that lucky.

My father spotted him coming out of a building at the far end of a row of buildings. He pointed at the man. "Christopher, I want you to go give the bullet back to that man."

I stared up at my father. I was nervous and very embarrassed. "Are you going to go with me?" I pleaded pathetically.

My dad shook his head. Looking at it from my age now, I think that both of us were in pain over my theft of the bullet. "This is something you are going to have to own up to on your own. You were the one who took the bullet. You are going to have to return it yourself without me." He pushed me forward in the direction of the man. Fear and embarrassment crashed over me like a large wave.

My tiny hand gripped the bullet and I walked hesitantly toward the man who seemed to get taller and larger the closer I got to him. As I reached the man, I looked up at him and smiled sheepishly. I was scared to death to be there and embarrassed to have to make my confession about stealing the bullet. He knelt down to hear me as the words choked their way out of my throat very quietly and jerky. "I'm sorry, Sir. I took one of the bullets from your belt." I barely got the words to pass my lips as I held up the bullet to him. I felt very small as the embarrassment seemed to weigh me down so heavily I thought I was being swallowed up by the ground beneath my feet.

He took the bullet from my hand. He smiled. "Thank you for being so honest. It took a great deal of courage for you to give this back by yourself."

I stared up at him. He was almost as tall as my father. "My father told me it was wrong to have taken it," I proudly proclaimed to the man whose bullet I had taken.

Standing up he took me by the hand and walked me back to my father who was smiling at my completion of my task. Actually I think he was laughing as his eyes sparkled and his mouth sported a small smile. At the time I was so relieved that the man wasn't angry, I didn't notice.

On the way back home in the car my father tried to explain to me the value of facing up to your responsibilities regardless of the situation. Looking back on that day I learned a great deal about facing up to the things I have to do. It's a good thing, too. In the course of my years on this earth I have fouled up a

My father took this photo of my sister and me. The horse's name was Stardust.

number of times where I had to face the consequences of my actions. If it were not for that lesson, I might be a whole lot less confident and sure of myself when life's situations have presented themselves. I learned to fail and to be human in my imperfection. Those facets are a part of the structure of achieving. They are hard lessons, to be sure, but valuable and very necessary. Those early lessons proved very valuable for me in later years when I would draw upon them for the courage necessary to contend with some of the problems I had.

****

You'll notice the conspicuous absence of references to my mother in this book. It's not that I have nothing to say about her; it's just that her private life is not a subject which I will include in this book other than in passing, or when it is necessary to illustrate a point about my father. I will say that she has been one of my most supportive and loving friends to this date. She also taught me a great deal about having a sense of humor

Randolph and Pat Scott at Trader-Vic's Restaurant in Beverly Hills

since she had a very devious and playful one. Her privacy is important to me and it is a trust I will not break for any reason.

It is worth noting that my mother spent her married life as my father's greatest fan, as well as acting as his secretary for more years than she cares to remember. To this day she still personally answers my father's fan mail. It's funny that many of the people who have been writing fan mail over the years have become good friends of the family, at least through the cards and letters. This is all a result of the personal role my mother took in my father's career and the lives of her children as well. Truth to tell, my Mom is the great organizer of the family. She used to drive me to distraction with her lists and notes, but she taught me the basics of my organizational skills. Actually I wish I'd learned her thoroughness and attention to detail a little better.

To my sister and me she has been nothing less than a sweet, caring and loving individual — not a perfect mother, as she makes mistakes like the rest of us, but one who I wouldn't ever want to trade in on a different model. I mention this just so that you will know that there is no "*Mommy Dearest*" story here, either. In a way it's sad to have to make a disclaimer of this type, but people being what they are, I figured I needed to do it.

****

In their mid-fifties most men are slowing the pace of their lives. Not so for Randolph Scott. His film making was in high gear with motion pictures such as *Sugarfoot, Santa Fe, Forth Worth, Man in the Saddle,The Man Behind the Gun, Carson City* and *The Stranger Wore a Gun*. His age seemed to matter little if at all to his audience. They only wanted to see another Randolph Scott Film. To them he was the same determined, straight-shooting hero they had always known. In many respects he was ageless.

Age, where it related to Randolph Scott as a father was a unique situation. Dad was born some fifty-two years before me, and I am the oldest of two children. You might think that that fact might have limited his participation in the games and sports in which we as children involved ourselves. Within limits I suppose that Dad's participation was more or less limited because of his age. More limiting was the fact that as an actor he was not home a great deal when there was a film to shoot. Still he missed very little of our lives due to the rigors of the shooting schedule. He always made time for us and involved himself fully in my sister's and in my life.

One drawback to his age was the reality that for all the years he was an actor he did the majority of his own stunts. I don't care how good you are — that has to take its toll on your body. It affects your back and your knees and sometimes just your general flexibility. I remember one film he did in the mid-1950s. It was called *The Tall-T*. Keep in mind that he was about fifty-seven years old at this time. One scene in the film required him to ride a Brahma bull. Now, I'm forty-three years old as I sit at my computer writing this, and I'm in reasonably good shape, but there is no way in hell that I'm going to jump on the back of a bull. I hope I am disciplined enough and lucky enough to be in as good a shape as my father was when I get into my late fifties and beyond. He looked better as he entered a room than many people my age now.

That incident cost him physically, although he came through it with no serious injury. Unfortunately that kind of stunt may have a cumulative effect on your body. After a while the full range of motion you enjoyed in your youth tends to become rather limited. This, of course, is on top of the limitations which age so graciously affords. When I was old enough to get hooked on playing basketball, my father was already in his sixties. He made sure that we had a proper basketball set-up, and he did his best to teach me how to play. It was less effort for most of my friends' fathers to teach them and join us in an occasional game, as they were considerably younger than my dad. It's funny, though, that in most cases it was my father who would forego some of his interests even though his time was

Age seemed irrelevant to Randolph Scott. Even in his late fifties he was doing his own stunt work.

more limited than many of those other fathers.

He may not have been able to slam-dunk a basketball or hit home runs like Willie Mays, but he was always behind me when it came to my education and sports. What he could not physically teach he coached from the edges of the court or sidelines. He knew the forms and the styles of almost every game I played with only a few exceptions. He encouraged me in sports in the same manner he had in scholastic proficiency. He believed that both were needed to be well rounded and capable.

He also saw my need to participate in sports at school. If he was home, he came to my games at school since I was on several varsity teams from the ninth grade forward. When I started surfing he would often take me to the beach so that I could take advantage of time and tide. I found out quite innocently in a conversation we had a few years before he passed away, that in those days he would find a spot on the beach where he felt I wouldn't see him and just watch. He must have hidden himself very well because I never had a clue that he was there. In a way it was a neat thing. I can just imagine my father in his suit or sports jacket, with his shoes and socks in his hand, standing under the cover of that old pier watching me surf. It is a rather humorous image but the fact is inescapably flattering. It shows a volume of interest in me of which I was unaware at the time.

I remember he was sitting in his favorite chair in the living room of the house where I was raised. I don't know if it was his favorite chair, but it was the one I recall him sitting in most often. When you walked into our living room you could see right away which seats my mother and father occupied. We were talking of the past as we waited for my mother to come and join us for dinner. He looked up at me with that knowing twinkle in his eyes. "You know it used to delight me to watch you surf when you were first learning," he confessed.

I was surprised. "What do you mean?" I asked.

He smiled. He was not well but his face seemed to light up as we spoke. "Do you remember the times when I took you to the Beach Club so that you could learn to surf?"

I nodded my head and listened very intently.

I know he didn't feel well, but he spoke with such fondness of the memory I couldn't very well cut him off. "At the northern end of the Beach Club property there was the remains of an old pier. I used to wait about twenty minutes after letting you off and then I'd walk down to that pier and I'd watch you. It made me very proud to watch you as you learned. I never stayed long, but it tickled me to watch you. I felt just like I did back when you learned to ride your bicycle." His smile broadened as his mind most likely jumped back to the time when I was learning to ride my bike.

"Why didn't you ever tell me?" I always thought I was pretty observant when I was at the beach in those days.

He shook his head, allowing his gaze to drift back to the scene outside the window. "I didn't want to embarrass you. Besides I didn't want to make you nervous. There were a few times . . ." He didn't finish the rest of his thoughts because my mother came into the room. I wanted to talk to him more about it, but after dinner he was tired and the opportunity never arose again before he passed away. There were some conversations which he believed belonged only between two people. It wasn't out of secrecy but out of a shared moment that he felt was personal and private. One to one moments like that tend to make you feel special anyway.

He always seemed so busy in his dealings with either motion pictures or business. It is nice to know I mattered to him. I'm sure he had more pressing matters on his mind. It was a part of him to act in this manner. He did what he did without fanfare or reward. Judging by just watching him he had the reward he most wanted. More so than many other parents he participated in and was part of all that we did — and like the example of surfing — sometimes we never knew. Maybe he felt I would be embarrassed if I knew. It is a fact I probably would have felt at least a little intimidated if I had known. I'm sure I would have tried to do my very best and most likely would have ended up falling off my board from trying too hard.

He pulled a stunt like that when I was in my early twenties. I had been asked by a teacher friend of mine to give a lecture on dolphins and whales to her oceanography class at UCLA. (Ruth Lebow was the woman whose Oceanography classes at Pierce College in the San Fernando Valley in the late 1960s inspired my thirst for knowledge and greater intimacy with the ocean.) At the time I was working at Sea World as well as studying the physiology and behavior of dolphins and whales quite intensively. This had been a consuming interest of mine for a number of years. Unknown to me, Ruth, the professor, invited my parents to attend. In those days I was still recovering from abject fear of speaking to groups of people. I'd had a stuttering problem for much of my adolescent life; and that is why, as I got older, I tried to force myself to speak to large groups of people in an attempt to overcome it. Working at Sea World and giving lectures gave me the perfect opportunity to force myself to come to terms with my nervousness and my stuttering.

Fortunately I have gotten over it very well, but this is divergent from the point. I spoke to Ruth's class for the better part of two hours. It took me the first five or ten minutes to get my stuttering under control but once I got into the swing of it, I spoke without hesitation or flaw. It was a large class so it was held in a lecture hall. As I passed among the students after I had finished my lecture and made my way to the door where Ruth was standing, I looked to her left and noticed that my mother and my father had been seated in the aisle seats of the back row. I couldn't believe I had been so wrapped up in my lecture that I didn't see them enter the auditorium.

I was surprised to see my parents. They were obvious in the crowd. My father had on a suit looking handsome as always. My mother had on a dress of one kind or another, but I learned a long time ago that no matter what she wears she looks stunning. I couldn't help thinking to myself that they made a striking couple even if they were my parents. "Hi. How long have you been here?" I asked.

Dad smiled at me. His eyes beamed as did my mother's. "We have been here the whole time." He got this impish look on his face. It is hard to describe, but it was as if he had gotten something past me mixed, with a smile of pride for what I had done. "We didn't want to make you nervous so we sat back here." Considerate as always. Not an action he had to think about, as it is with so many people, but one of ingrained reflex. He wanted to share this moment and at the same time not embarrass me.

I used to get on my father's case occasionally for embarrassing me in public because of the way he acted towards me. I smiled at him at that moment. Many years have passed since he has been gone; I don't think I truly appreciated how much it mattered to him about the things which I did. I realize it now and I guess that is the important part.

My dad had a way of smiling at me when I did something right or exceptional, as he did that day of the lecture. That smile always made me feel very special. He would get a bright twinkle in his eyes and a sort of cat-who-ate-the-canary grin. Randolph Scott was not a terribly demonstrative man, but when he was pleased with something, it was evident on his face. It radiated from him. It was a condition I tried sometimes too hard to duplicate at different times in my life. Sometimes it is hard to realize the value that those who love you and care about you find in you. I tried so hard to excel thinking that was what my father wanted from me, and it turns out he would have been just as pleased regardless of what I did. Go figure.

****

Dad may not have been able to actively participate in many of the contact sports which I chose to play; but he was more than happy to spend time playing golf with me at any opportunity. Golf was his passion. He worked and crafted his skills on the links in much the same way an artist or a sculptor might work at honing his or her skills. I used to watch him practice his golf stroke with utter fascination when I was only a few years old. It was kind of like watching a sculptor. Each stroke of his club chipped away toward the perfection of his game. Feet slightly apart, shoulders in line with the target and his grip firm and perfect on the club — It couldn't have been more perfect.

Now I grew up in Beverly Hills, and our house sat on a

reasonable amount of land. — In other words, the right side of the tracks (or maybe, the right side of the right side of the tracks). Most of our friends and our neighbors had swimming pools as well as large well-landscaped backyards. Some of the more pretentious houses which I visited or frequented as a child had tennis courts, but absolutely none of them had a putting green except ours. (From time to time I wonder what kind of a trade-off my father made to my mother so that he could destroy the symmetry of the backyard for his putting green. Knowing my mother, on the other hand, she wouldn't have denied him anything, especially when it came to his golf game.) Most people enjoy certain sports and participate in them as often as is reasonable. My father was not just a golf enthusiast; he was totally committed to the game. The only thing in his life which took precedence over his passion for the game was his family and the business he maintained to sustain us.

Since golf played such an important role in my father's life, it was natural that as soon as I was old enough to understand the rules I learned to play. For a child that is exactly what it is . . . playing. Some of the game was taught to me by the local golf pro at whatever place we were staying. The rest was taught to me by my father who was most often a better golfer than the club pros. In my early teens when we vacationed at the Eldorado Country Club in Palm Desert, I used to play occasionally with him. God, he was an annoying man on the course! He was never satisfied with his performance. Most people who play golf would give almost anything to shoot par. Not my father. He said that to be the best you had to look at your performance and realize that it could always be better. He actually used to get mad at himself if he missed dipping under par and had to settle for par. Settle for par?! Hell, I'd have been glad on some of those holes to be one or two over par!

I believe the thirteenth hole at the Eldorado Country Club is the par five that leads toward the club and away from the surrounding hills, which make the Eldorado so picturesque. It is a long par five. On this particular occasion I was fifteen years old and we were in the desert for Christmas vacation. My father's drive was flawless and had good distance. (He couldn't take a full swing at the ball as injuries to his back kept him from the last ten to twenty percent of a normal swing. Even with his reduced swing he was more than capable of pressing three hundred yards on his tee shots.) If he could get a solid hit on his second shot, he would be on the green and he would one putt for two under par. That's impressive. More impressive if not for the fact that he played like that all the time. He lined up the shot and swung. "Judas Priest!" He cursed under his breath. He had flubbed the shot. Instead of being on the green he was just short, which was perfect position for him to birdie the hole.

I walked over to him. "Great shot, Dad", I said with envy in my voice.

He stared at me for not understanding his feelings for his poor performance. "I didn't hit that very well." He was aggravated at himself for the next two holes because he did not get two under par.

I tried my best to make him feel better, but he was a perfectionist about this game. "Come on, Dad. Almost nobody gets two under on this hole." When he missed and knew that it should have been better, he would repeat it in his mind trying to correct the mistake. That's what used to annoy me about playing golf with him. There was absolutely no way to compete. It would be like being Dennis Conner's son and going out for a friendly race. (Remember that my passion is sailing. That is why I used this example.)

Palm Desert in those days had a fair share of celebrity pro/amateur golf tournaments and my father was always one of the first to enter if we were going to be in the desert. Trust me, we were always in the desert at those times. In the early sixties I recall one of the Bob Hope Desert Classics. Dad was paired with Billy Casper's foursome. I was in my early teens. Ordinarily I had better things to do than to follow my father and the other golfers around the course. On this day, however, I was at a loss for entertainment so I decided to watch my father's foursome.

To my understanding at the time the best played shot is the one the rest of the players use as opposed to playing their own.

I got quite a chuckle out of the fact that, more often than not, it was my father's shot that was used in deference to the position of the two pros who were playing with him. Billy Casper would glance over at my father, who was lining up the differences between the lay of the balls. He waved at my father more than half the time that it would be his shot that would be used. Dad would acknowledge the nod with an almost modest wave of his hand. Billy Casper just smiled like, "Oh well." It was nice to know that I wasn't the only one who had to contend with my father's unerring ability to hit and place the ball.

****

Growing up can be difficult regardless of who your parents are and without respect to their social and economic status. Your sense of identity can — and most often is — a source of constant flux as a result of social pressure and your internal sense of belonging. This sense can be jeopardized further if you are adopted.

Yes, I am adopted. I'm not exactly sure of the reason my parents couldn't have their own children; but suffice it to say, they were unable to have their own biological offspring. Actually even if I knew the reason, I would most likely not share it as it is information you do not need to understand the subject of this book.

As I said, it might be more or less traumatic to find out that you are not really your parents' child in a biological sense anyway. You might wonder who your real parents were. Why they chose not to keep you for themselves. Through the years there have been an ad nauseam number of talk shows dedicated to that very topic. I guess I was very lucky in that respect. As far back as I can remember my mother and my father told both my sister and me that we were adopted. I think the difference between me and other adopted children was the warm and loving way in which I was told.

I recall my mother used to tell me. "We picked out you specially. When we wanted your sister we took you with us and you helped pick her out."

"Did you really pick us out?" I remember asking that of my father when I was a small child filled with questions.

He would smile and nod his head. "You were exactly the children we wanted; that's why we adopted you." The answer was less important than the genuine affection and love which littered and insinuated his words. It was tender. The emotion was unmistakable.

I remember feeling very special when he told me. It never occurred to me that someone didn't want me, which is the way many adopted children seem to attribute their adoptive circumstance. Many times, couples have children because it just happens and by moral decree or human acceptance, they keep the child even though they may not really have wanted it. My parents wanted to have a child and they chose me. That's all I knew. Someone wanted me enough to go down and pick me out themselves.

Looking back I doubt very much that that was true, but at the time it served to make me at least feel very special. I never felt cheated or different in any way that Randolph and Patricia Scott were my parents. Quite the contrary I felt unique and special about it. I guess it was the way they handled the subject. It also speaks well of the love and devotion they gave me and each other. I know that there are large numbers of adopted children who feel much differently about that subject.

In the 1970s there was a large movement for people to get in touch with their roots. That was when so many adopted children were steamed up and ready to find their biological parents. For me I never really thought twice about it. My real parents were the two people who shared all the failures and the successes of my life from my very first memory to the present. I can't for the life of me understand why I would look for something else in two people whom I had never even met. My parents were those people who held me when I was sick and who basically shared my life and stood by me. They held my hand when I was sick and stayed by me until I was well. OK, Mom never made me the soup but she had the cook make it. At least she was the one who brought it to me, and she was also the one who went to the store and purchased the ingredients.

Now I'm sure that through the early years of my life my parents must have wondered if they had done the right thing by adopting me. I know I was a terror with a boundless and limitless supply of energy. I have been introspective at times and, quite honestly, I could have been a much better child. There were times over the years that I was a major league pain in the ass. As children go I have known much better. I guess at times I wondered if I was ever a disappointment to them. I caused more than my share of problems and stirred up far more than my share of negative emotions in them as I was growing up.

A few years before my father passed away we were sitting in the living room drinking a beer. Even then his health was beginning to decline. He was looking a little thin and gaunt. In any event we were alone at that particular moment. My mom was in her room getting ready to come to dinner and she was well out of ear shot. My father and I had a very rocky road to travel through the years. He had never wavered in his support of me, but I know that at times it must have been very hard for him. Even though our horns locked through the years my love for him and his for me was strong. I guess at that time I was feeling a bit insecure about his feelings for me. It was nothing he had expressed to me. It was just that I was feeling insecure about me and my future.

I don't know why I chose that moment to put a question to him. "Dad, this is a bad question, but was it worthwhile to have adopted me?" I asked, pensive and frightened to hear his reponse.

He looked puzzled that I asked the question. He cleared his throat and then looked at me. "You haven't always been the easiest son to have gotten along with, but you have had your moments. I don't think I would rather have had any other son. There have been a great number of times when you have made me very proud." There was a tear in his eye as he spoke. " Sometimes you just try too hard to get to the end result. I just want you to be all that you can be. I have tried my best to teach you everything you need to know." He smiled and blinked back the small tear. "You can be far more than you realize, Son. As long as you are doing your best I will always be proud and happy that I adopted you. Even with all the problems I have never been anything but glad that you are my son." He reached over and squeezed my hand. My father was not overly demonstrative but he never failed to show his affection and his love in the way he communicated with me.

The emotion of that moment has stayed with me ever since. I may never have been the boy he wanted, but I have always tried to be the man he taught me to be. I have fallen short of my expectation far too often in that pursuit, but as I grow older I find that I am more capable of achieving the kind of balance in my life that my father tried so hard to teach me when he was alive.

We had a number of father and son discussions throughout the years. Some were very positive, but all too often they served to remind me that I needed to follow my father's advice and teaching a little more closely. I hated to fail and sometimes I went too far in my efforts to avoid that sense of failure. It goes back to learning the lessons my father tried to give me about patience and taking things one step at a time.

I was disheartened in my early twenties as things in my life were not going as I had intended. My father sat me down on the soft brown ottoman in his room. "You know, Chris, not everything that you plan is going to work the way you plan it." I recall he smiled. That smile conveyed his understanding more eloquently than any words could have. "The difference between success and failure is the lessons you learn from the experience. Failure simply increases the likelihood that the next time you will accomplish what you wanted but first you must take the time to analyze what it was that caused you not to succeed." My father had been a very successful man in his lifetime. When he spoke to me at times like this he was absolute in his sincerity. It was in his eyes. They spoke gentle volumes about his intentions and his feelings. He wanted to help me through the rough spots by sharing the expanse of his wisdom and experience.

****

It is tradition in many families for the ever-dutiful sons to venture into the professions which are chosen for them by the family, or more specifically, the father. I'm glad that my father had no aspirations for me to follow his lead in the movie business. I have to admit, however, that there were a few times in my life when I gave it more than a little thought. Most often he told me empathetically not to even think about it. Of course that didn't mean that he didn't have other ideas for the directions my life should follow. I know I had conversations and arguments with my father about following courses he so carefully set out for me. While many of my friends had been compliant enough to have done as their father's had wished, I was different

In analyzing my own past and some of the decisions I had made, I'm not totally sure I was a rebel because of conviction or because I just had to go against the flow. There were times when I'm very sure one or the other was true and more limited times when both were valid at the same time. There were more than a few times when my father and I would lock horns because his idea of a course for my life diverged most dramatically from the course I had chosen.

The summer I turned twenty my father and I had gotten into a horrendous argument. I'm kind of glad that my mother was out of the house shopping at the time because my father and I both said some things which were less than complimentary about each other. It's a good thing that neither of us are physical individuals because this particular argument was intense enough and heated enough to have come to blows if either of us had had the inclination.

It's funny that I have never ever been able to remember the specifics of the bad things which have happened to me, but I can be most specific about the good times. I'm sure it goes back to my father's philosophy that one should learn from the bad but cherish the good. Anyway we were locked in a tremendous argument. He wanted me to do one thing and I was bound and determined to stay the course I was already taking. We argued for the better part of two hours.

I wanted to get my point of view across to my father. "Look!

You have your way of looking at the issue. That doesn't mean that my view isn't valid," I urged with great passion in my voice.

Dad was definitely angry which didn't happen very often, but he was not going to agree with me. "Christopher, I told you that I will not allow you to do this. It's not right. You should be more like Craig Gosden. (Craig Gosden was the son of my father's friend Freeman Gosden, who was the originator of "The Amos and Andy Show" on radio as well as television. Craig and I were very good friends as well.) Craig does exactly what his father wants him to do." His eyes were ablaze as he spoke.

In my younger days I had the capacity for having a very bad temper coupled with a tendency to have my feelings hurt very easily. Both factors snapped me fully open at that moment. My heart sank and my fists clenched. It took every bit of my control to keep from lashing out in the manner which my more primitive emotions screamed to my body. I stared coldly at my father. I was hurt and angry. "Would you respect me if I just complacently did all that you asked of me without making allocation for my own beliefs and feelings? Would it be better if I were the clay figure that you wanted me to be?"

He stepped back from me. You could see the anger in his eyes replaced by thought and his contemplation of my question. The fire went out of him as he shook his head. "No, I wouldn't respect you as much if you just blindly did what I asked of you. I'm your father, Chris." There was anguish in his voice at the frustration of trying to do the right thing by me but not getting it through to me. "It is my responsibility to look out for you and to try and guide you away from problems. I don't want you to do everything I ask. I just want to save you from as much heartache and pain as I can. I have had a great deal more experience than you."

We shook hands and embraced. We then apologized for the things we had said to each other. There was room in my father's and my opinions for differences. The bottom line was that even though we could heatedly disagree, there was an underlying respect for each other. Thank God. We were able to talk more constructively after that moment and actually resolved the conflict which had started the argument in the first place.

I think that's one of the things I respected most about my father. He could be stern and rigid at times, and occasionally the two of us together were like two bulls battling for dominance. Through it all, however, there was never a time when I felt that he didn't love me or didn't care about me. That means something very special to me. I have known many people in my time and very few of them have the capability to be angry and yet still show that they love you. I've tried through my life to be one of those who can approximate that skill.

****

I caused my father great consternation about my education all through the years of my schooling and then some. He knew my capabilities, but for a long period of time in my youth he was at a loss as to the most effective way of motivating me. My mother and he tried threats, punishments, withholding almost anything and even hired a teacher to tutor me. I wasn't really a bad student. I didn't fail any classes but I was severely under motivated. English and mathematics seemed to be my worst subjects. I am sure I will never know the lengths to which my father went to try to find some way or someone to motivate me because he isn't alive any longer. He did, however, whether intentional or unintentional, find a way to get me on the right track.

Manning O'Connor lived two doors down the street from our house. The O'Connors had three sons. One was my age, and the other two were well into their college years by the time I was twelve years old. Dad was never one not to take advantage of an opportunity when it presented itself. By accident, Dad heard the two older O'Connor boys speaking to a friend of theirs who was a student at Loyola University. He was an English major but he was also well schooled in mathematics. To my father he seemed the answer to a prayer. The student's name was Brian Fay.

Brian needed supplementary income, and he was nothing

like any of the other tutors whom my father had tried before, so they struck a deal. It worked out quite nicely. For the two years while Brian and I were acquainted, we extended our relationship far beyond that of tutor and student. We became good friends.

The day Brian was to begin tutoring me Dad walked into my room. It was a Monday and I had just gotten back from school. I looked up at my father as he walked in. "Hi, Dad," I greeted him.

My father wasn't smiling. He had on his dark gray suit which made him look even more serious to me. "I spoke to your principal last week and he tells me that you are still having difficulty in English and Algebra."

I nodded my head. I would have commented, but it was obvious that my father knew the facts so I said nothing.

Taking my silence as acceptance my father continued, "I've asked a friend of Pat O'Conner's to stop by today to talk to you about tutoring. His name is Brian Fay. He is an honor student at Loyola University. I think he'll be able to help you if you give him a chance." Dad walked over to the chair at my desk and sat down. "Your education is very important, Son. I want you to have every possible chance to get a good one. Brian is very sharp. I think you and he will get along so give him a chance for me, won't you?"

"Sure, Dad." I knew I needed help in my studies. I didn't lack the intelligence but I lacked the motivation. Still, an honor student? In my mind that conjured up some brainy-looking character with a pocket protector and really thick glasses. Fortunately for me that is not how Brian turned out to be.

Perspective is a wonderful thing to possess if you are a parent. I think my dad had perspective. He must have; otherwise I don't think he would have had the sense of humor necessary to allow his teenage son to hang around with a college senior. I know if I were a parent I might have some very strong reservations about letting my child be exposed to a more accelerated lifestyle than one ordinarily finds in high school and junior high school. Oddly, Dad found Brian to be an excellent choice of friends. He was a good person for me to use as a model. The proof of that is that many of the life lessons I acquired under Brian are still within me today.

Without my friendship with Brian I think that I would never have experienced Bach or Stravinsky. I might never have had the sensation of power and passion of LeMer or Afternoon of a Fawn. Certainly I might not have been as good with people as I have become without the lessons I received from Brian.

As I think back on the time I spent with Brian Fay I wonder just how my father knew that I would hit it off with Brian. How did he seem to know that Brian could reach me when he and so many others had failed? Actually he seemed to know quite a lot about people and things, but he rarely let on. Randolph Scott was a quiet, thoughtful person. Even though he was significantly older than the parents of most of my friends, his ability to see into the future for the right solutions and courses of action was amazing.

In retrospect I think my father knew intuitively that Brian could give me many of the things that he couldn't. While Brian was not that much older than me he had many of the qualities which my father possessed. My father was a great deal older than me, being closer in age to a grandfather than a father. Physically, there were some things he couldn't do. Some of these things Brian could and did for me. The lessons he taught me were invaluable, but at the same time, they were lessons which my father knew I needed as well.

****

As I said earlier if I had had a teenage son, I don't think I would have allowed, much less encouraged, a friendship with a college student in his early twenties. For a number of reasons and especially the fact that drinking is far more likely in college students than in high school students, my father already had that battle out of the way before I entered my teens. Both my sister and I were allowed a certain small liberty when it came to alcohol. My father and my mother wanted to make sure that having a beer or a drink was little else than a pleasant diversion. So we were taught the responsibility of drinking.

If I wanted to have a portion of beer with my father before dinner he allowed it, not all the time, but occasionally. As a consequence when I was around alcohol at parties or functions, it was not the big deal as I have seen it be to so many others whose parents were non-communicative about the subject. I really have appreciated my parents' wisdom about alcohol since then. It has never been a big deal. The primary reason was the manner in which it was treated in our house from the time my sister and I were quite young. It was a good lesson. To my knowledge neither my sister nor myself have ever abused liquor.

Even though it has been more than twenty-five years since my father last spoke to me about the responsibilities of drinking, I can still see him and hear him.

We were sitting in the living room. I had come by the house to visit before going somewhere. My father looked at me as I sipped the beer which I had procured from the bar. "Son, I hope you are aware of the responsibility of drinking. If you are the one driving and you are going out, it is your responsibility. It doesn't matter how much the people who are with you are drinking, it is your responsibility to stay aware and sober. Even if you are not the one who drove you have to be responsible enough to make sure that you are able to drive if the others cannot." I remember he shook his head and looked very seriously at me. "Do not ever get into a car where the driver has been drinking too much or if you have been drinking too much. You call me from wherever you are, and I will come and get you or arrange to get you home. Please, Son, it is not worth your life to be on the road in that condition."

I remember smiling at him and nodding my affirmation. "Thanks, Dad." I hugged him for his concern and left. Those words have stayed with me since then. It wasn't the words exactly, but the passion which lay below them as he spoke them. Keep in mind that this occurred long before Mothers Against Drunk Drivers came into existence

I think Dad wanted us to have control over a substance which has exerted control over so many other people, both young and old. It is a lesson I have taken with me into a number of other areas of my life. I have watched what that lack of control with liquor and drugs has done to a number of my friends over the years. I have even lost a few friends to the idiotic impairment which comes over people when they drink and drive. Every time I see someone overcome by alcohol I pause a moment and thank my father for the wisdom and judgment he afforded me when I was young. (Yes, I do drink. I drink beer and an occasional shot of Tequila. I just don't get sloppy falling down drunk.) My father taught me well the lessons of moderation, especially where it relates to drinking.

There was one time when I was young that I overindulged in drinking. It was a first experimentation. The house, mansion actually, which was next door to us belonged to the Meyers. The Meyers' grandson and I were friends. At the times when he stayed with his grandparents we would get together. Buried deep within the bowels of the house was a wine cellar which was barred by a vault door with a huge combination lock. From the time Addison and I were nine years old we tried to figure out the combination. It was a harmless recreation until I got to the age of thirteen. That year, Addison and I got into the vault. We also got into several expensive bottles of wine.

Since we had a party in the back of the Meyers' house, Addison and I split our treasure drinking the spoils of our conquest. I thought the liquor didn't affect me. I guess I was wrong because when I came home and said goodnight to my mother she insisted that I go in and give my father a kiss goodnight. "Chris, you go in a say good night to your father. Make sure you give him a big hug and a kiss." I don't remember much of that event for obvious reasons. I think my mother was chuckling.

I walked on unsteady legs into my father's room. "Good night, Dad." I gave him a big hug and a kiss.

Because of my condition I don't recall exactly what his expression was but I have a pretty good idea. His eyebrows were raised and I'm sure he looked askance at me as he lay in his massive bed which was custom made for him. It was at least a few percent bigger in all directions than the largest king-size. I know he smiled. "Did you have a good time with

Addison?"

I was probably slurring my words, but I thought I was being quite coherent at the time. "Yeah, Dad. I sure did."

My father snickered for a moment and then, as I recall, smiled so broadly that it had to have hurt. "Well, you go to bed, Son. Be careful getting to your room." He leaned over to my mother. "Pat, make sure he gets to his room, please."

My mother complied. She didn't say anything although I believe she wanted to say something. I think she might have wanted to call me on the fact that I had been drinking, but my father didn't. I stumbled to my room. The next morning I knew exactly why my father hadn't scolded me the night before. I was in major-league pain. My head hurt and my mouth tasted as if an army of dirty people had trudged through it. Even my eyes hurt. I remember walking out to have breakfast. I didn't feel like eating, but it was expected that I be polite and sit with my parents. I walked into the lanai very slowly and thankful that our house was a quiet place.

My father was already seated at the table. He was dressed in a tweed sport coat. He looked up only briefly from his newspaper and cup of coffee as I sat down at the table. "Did you have a good time last night, Chris?" He put down his paper and looked at me.

The lanai is the room we used to eat lunch and dinner. It was right by the pool and two full walls were floor-to-ceiling glass. The sun was particularly brilliant that morning, and I had to blink frequently to keep the glare from burning out my brain. "Yeah, Dad. We had a great time."

He smiled that "Boy, did you do the wrong thing" smile at me. "Next time you'll be sure not to do that, won't you?" He picked his paper back up and continued reading.

My head hurt enough, and now I was embarrassed. "Yeah, Dad." Now I fully understood. There was no punishment in the world which would have made me feel worse. I looked up at him. He had a rather smug smile on his face as he read the paper. "Is it all right with you if I go back to my room?" I was praying he would say yes.

He looked over the top of his glasses at me. "Certainly." He smiled impishly. "But I want you to start on your homework. I'll be over later to check on you."

I walked slowly back to my room. It took me hours to get over that feeling. What was worse was the fact that my father knew exactly what he was doing. I learned my lesson from it, so I guess he knew what he was doing.

I never saw my father really drunk. He was never drunk in the way we seem to picture someone when that comment is made. There was one New Year's Eve I remember quite well. We were celebrating in the dining room of the Eldorado Country Club in Palm Desert. It was one of the only times I ever saw my father tipsy from drinking too much. He sat in his chair with a silly smile on his face. He wasn't loud or aggressive. He just looked . . . happy. From the way he acted at that time you could have asked him anything and he would have been agreeable.

The only other time I can recall him drinking too much was at my first wedding. He and my best friend Robb Bacon took it upon themselves to pass around the bottles of champagne. They both drank less than three glasses, but they ended up looking like two of the silliest people. By the end of the reception they were sitting next to each other on the couch. My father was holding a glass in one hand and a bottle of champagne in the other, and Robb was just holding a glass. Neither was speaking; they just watched the people and smiled. It wasn't offensive; it was cute, if anything. They didn't bother anybody. They were both suited rubbery statues who had silly grins attached to their faces.

****

There are times when some people like to use their position and fame to further themselves with trivial or quasi-lofty pursuits. I know most everyone has experienced this at least once in their lives if not substantially more. All of us have heard the lines. "Do you know who I am?" "My father is an important man in this town." Or even worse, they trade off their reputation like the more common among us owe them something just because they deigned to speak to us or enter our store. That is one of the things I hated about Beverly Hills. There were so many people who had over inflated egos about their relative importance to those around them.

Character is wonderful quality if you have it. Most of those who act as above, are truly lacking in that particular asset. My father never had that problem. Yes, he was very well known but he didn't trade on it. Certainly there were times when he may have been treated better or more quickly than a more average man but it was never expected. This is important. He never really expected it. It was his manners and his humility which prevailed in these situations.

Ah yes, I remember the lectures very well that Dad used to give me about telling people who I was. He would stand in front of me his brow furrowed in concern. "It is better if you do not tell people who you are or what family you are from until you get to know them. It may gain you some superficial respect but it doesn't mean anything. It is better for people to know you for who you are inside. Besides there are far too many people out there who will take advantage of you if they think you have money or belong to an important family."

Randolph Scott was an important and busy figure in the community where we lived. You would never have seen him push to the front of a line to be waited on or to be served first. Now there are those who I have seen in my lifetime who are far less noteworthy than my father, and who strutted around pushing people out of the way as if it should be expected as their right. Not my father. On occasion a person where he was shopping or eating would offer to allow him ahead of others, but most times he would smile slightly and decline. He didn't mind waiting his turn. I think it embarrassed him when people treated him that way.

In some ways I think people extended certain courtesies to my father because of the respect he engendered in them. If he had expected those people to go out of their way for him, I think, it might not have been so frequent and genuine in appearance. He was, after all, a modest and unassuming man. The fact that he stood out and was easily recognizable was more physiology and demeanor than bravado or arrogance.

"Good manners will get you farther in this life with other people than all the money in the world. Manners and courtesy will bring you far more rewards. They will build a reputation for you of which most people will be envious." He believed that and it was an important lesson for me to have learned.

He never approached a hostess or maitre de of a restaurant and announced his identity. Granted, most people in the years when I grew up probably could recognize him on sight. If there was a wait before we could be seated or if a salesperson was busy, he politely waited his turn with no fuss and certainly never any negative comments. He expected the same from his children. I learned a great deal from him just by following his examples.

Some of the kids with whom I used to associate in those years didn't think twice about using their families' influence to further themselves. I guess there were times when I tried to do the same thing. In those instances my father let me know in no uncertain terms that it was inappropriate behavior and that he wouldn't tolerate it. To my father it was important that my sister and I be known and respected for ourselves. He felt it absolutely imperative that we develop our own way of achieving instead of always relying on his name to get us through.

More than a few of the people we knew in our youth traded on their parents' fame to further themselves. Whether they used that name to open doors or to get a start in the movie business, it really didn't matter. The reality was they were not doing it on their own merits but allowing themselves to be swept in by respect and reputation built by their parents. Dad would never approve of either my sister or me trading or furthering ourselves as a result of his fame or reputation.

A light may be going on for some of you. Yes, by writing this book I am within limits trading off my father's name but not in the way you might think. No doubt It will do well as I think most people are interested in the lives of prominent figures. What you may not realize is that I am less concerned with the monetary aspect of this book than I am with sharing some of the life and stories I experienced in my time with my father. There have already been a number of other books published about him. A few have been more or less factual biographies. One or two have been rather derogatory, and to my way of thinking, completely out of line in their comments. I just want to share a little of the memories I cherish about a man who is well known from a very personal point of view. Randolph Scott was a very complex and compassionate man. He believed in some very specific things, and I think that those things are worth sharing. They were, after all, the things that made him the man that he was, and that is a story worth sharing. Actually, I think he might like what I have tried to accomplish in this book.

In looking back I have some understanding of my father's sentiments about being famous and well known. He made his way in life on his own terms. Through his own unique style and civility he created a niche for himself in movies. Most of them are still being shown on television so that current generations can share in his efforts. He believed in his work, but I doubt if he ever saw it as any different than other person who is at the top of his field. Acting — and in later years business — was his job. I can't remember him speaking of or desiring any awards for his contributions other than the satisfaction of doing the job he was given to the very best of his ability. I recall that he refused a number of awards in the time I was growing up. It wasn't a big deal to him as it might be to some others. Doing the job well and providing a good life for his family were his rewards. In that light it isn't a great stretch to see why even he refused to pass himself off as self-important. It is less of a stretch to understand why he wouldn't want his children to ride his fame as well. He wanted us to be recognized for the people we are and not because of his name and fame. Through the passage of the years I have found that he was more than a little correct in his view and his assessment of people and the importance of personal reputation and achievement.

Chapter 3

PRACTICE
AND
PASSION

Everyone has a few things in his or her life that he or she really likes to do. I know I do. A relatively small percentage of people, it seems, takes this like of a particular activity or diversion and boosts it to the level of an all-consuming passion. Passion and the pursuit of passion was one of the cornerstones of Randolph Scott's personality and character. There were a few activities in his life which consumed him, and they insinuated into all facets and corners of his life. I love this part of this book because it had the greatest impact on my own life. Sounds serious, doesn't it? Or maybe it's an endorsement for his beliefs and philosophies — what do you think? Actually, it's less an invocation than an adherence to a basic style of looking at life and the things I or we do within it.

****

The house my father built in Beverly Hills was at the end of a dead-end street. On a street where most of the houses are two story ours was one story. No walls surrounded it, but the way the roof extends over the driveway and the way the plants grow, it is virtually invisible from the street. The backyard was large but not ostentatious as are so many of the mansions that litter the landscape in that city. Note the way I refer to my father's and my family's dwelling place as a house and not a mansion. A mansion was the building next door which had two floors, a basement and a sub-basement. It is a holdover from the time when Mexico still held sway over California. It was elaborate and cold.

Our house was just as it sounds . . . a house that was home to the Scott family. The inside was warm and comfortable, due

This is the house my father built.

in large part to the way my mother decorated and appointed it. The rich wood of the front door and elegant entry is humanized by the small upholstered bench where most often my mother left her keys and whatever packages and letters she did not want to forget. The living room was a symphony of earth tones in the carpet as well as in the furniture. Impressionistic paintings as well as a number of portraits graced the walls of that room and the solarium which served as ante-room to my parents' bedrooms. Pictures of friends and family adorned every table as do the ornamental ashtrays and the ornate cigarette lighters. It was not the traditional Beverly Hills interior that, while stylish and elegant, was sterile, cold and completely uninviting. In our house there was a warmth which came over you the moment you walked through that massive wooden front door and stayed with you in all rooms in the house. Yes, it looked as if we had money, but it also was friendly like my parents and inviting to the senses.

My father was a golf fanatic. He was not like other men although I am sure there are some who share his fervor for the game. Golf for him was an all encompassing passion that seemed at times to be his sole reason for living.

That passion was obvious in his character in *Coroner Creek*. He plays a rancher who swears vengance against the bandits responsible for his wife's death during a stagecoach robbery. Even though his vendetta nearly killed him he would not relent until he had exacted justice from the men who had caused him such pain. His determination as portrayed on the screen was the same as the determination he brought to his life off the screen. While some may be satisfied with a good performance in any given aspect of their lives Randolph Scott would settle for nothing less than his best.

This may have been the reason he selected this site for our house since the backyard portion of the lot was bordered all the way along the back by the third green and the fourth tee of the north course of the Los Angeles Country Club. (It might be fair

Mom and Dad in back of their cottage at the Eldorado Country Club in Palm Desert (1981)

to note that years later my father was permitted a membership to that club. He was the first, and, to my knowledge, the only actor who has ever been allowed to achieve that distinction. From what I was told he was given special allocation to join because of his character and reputation. I would elaborate, but I think I have already sufficiently covered that aspect of him.)

Golf, as many of you who play the game will attest, is not a sport where one buys the equipment and then plays. No, golf is a lifelong pursuit in frustration and of achievement. To illustrate my point just watch any golfer when he gets into the sand trap. A golfer crafts his game. In the beginning we are all duffers. Some, however, practice and study the rules and the courtesies until the completed function at the end of your life is an art form worthy of any of the past masters of any true art form. Of course, to the vast majority of golfers, it is just a game. Randolph Scott treated golf more seriously than the average person. To him it was more than just a game. Just playing was never his function. He endeavored to make each shot and each swing better. Many of his friends can attest to this fact, as well as to the pains he took in practicing and shaping the art form.

My family was in Palm Desert at the Eldorado Country Club for Christmas vacation. My father and I decided we would play a round of golf together which was something we tried to do at least a few times each vacation. We were due to tee off at noon. I arrived a little early which is not usual for me. It was a few minutes after eleven so I bought a bucket of balls at the driving range that I felt was necessary as a warm up before I played. I saw that my dad had the same idea except instead of taking his balls to the driving range, he walked over to the practice sand trap. I was amazed at this. My father has one of the best sand trap shots that I have ever seen, and here he is in the sand trap practicing.

I walked over to the sand trap after I finished my bucket of golf balls. I watched mesmerized as he swung his club. Each ball lifted out of the trap in an explosion of sand. The white ball arced into the air and toward the practice green as perfectly as I have ever witnessed. "Hey, Dad. Are you ready?" I was impatient, as always.

He looked away from his game long enough to smile and answer. "Let me just finish this bucket of balls, Chris." He had that damn smile on his face again. At this time in my life that smile was a red flag that warned me that some point was coming. I hated that. He had something rolling around in his mind, and I just knew he was waiting for the perfect moment to let go of it.

"Looks to me as if your sand trap shots are about as good as they can be." I started to walk toward the first tee.

My dad yelled to me from the trap, "Chris, why don't you finish this bucket for me while I get a new glove at the pro shop?"

I turned and looked at him questioningly. "Why? My sand trap shots are pretty good."

He laughed and reached into my bag drawing out my sand wedge. "Here." He handed it to me. "I've seen your trap shots, Son." He walked away chuckling to himself for his cuteness. I have to give him credit; his timing was incredible as was the impish manner which preceded it as well as followed it.

I took the club and pouted my way to the sand trap. After I finished the bucket of balls I joined my father at the first tee. The wind grazed his hair as he waited for me by the ball washer. We were an interesting pair. He in his gray slacks and ironed golf shirt and me in my shorts and T- shirt. I stared at him as I approached him. "Why did you want me to practice in the trap?"

"Your game is weak in that area." He spoke to me as he washed off and then towel dried his ball for use on the first hole. When he finished, he walked over to me. "Practice is the only way to be good at anything, Son. If you are going to play the game, you better be able to make the shots. It's good to have a strong drive and knock the ball three hundred yards or so down the fairway, but this game is won in the short game. The sand trap is your weak area."

God, I hated when he did that to me. He was, of course, correct as well. I treat sailing the way he treated golf, or as most of my friends will tell you I'm equally the pain in the backside in that forum as my father was in his.

My father was so serious about the game that he brought

it home with him. I must have been about four or five years old at the time when I first realized that something was going to be different about our backyard. I walked out of the lanai, which is a glass-walled room laying adjacent to the pool, and consequently into the backyard. I saw a couple of men smoothing a more or less circular section of the yard just a short distance from the swimming pool. There was no grass where they worked. I sat and watched them for a few hours until my mother called me to come in and to wash up for lunch.

We sat at the table in the lanai. No one seemed to be curious about the work that was still being carried out a number of yards from our table. We were still eating lunch when the rumbling vibrations of a large truck broke the tranquillity of the noon hour. My dad smiled at my mother like a child who has been given a giant box to open at Christmas and politely excused himself. He walked a little more quickly than I had seen him in the past. I didn't see him again until later that afternoon. I was curious about the noise so I walked to the front of the house after I had finished eating my lunch. There I saw a crew of men unloading large brown rolls from the truck and carrying them around to the back. I would have followed them as my curiosity was more than a little peaked, but my mother snagged me at that moment.

I don't remember what my mother had me do for the next hour, but it was at least that long before I could get to the backyard. I think she wanted to keep a tight leash on my natural curiosity and to keep me out of the way. The brown rolls I had seen the men carrying from the truck were actually sod. Not just any kind of grass, mind you, but the kind that is used for putting greens. I arrived just in time to watch the last two pieces of sod being gently laid out.

My father was grinning from ear to ear as he inspected the green. He thanked the men for their efforts on his behalf, and they left. He was gracious to the men, but I think he couldn't wait for them to be gone so that he could be alone with his new toy. He stood for a few moments inspecting the green and then walked to one side of the new green where a pile of stakes and a hammer were lying on the ground. My father took a number of stakes from the pile and picked up the hammer. He gently tapped them into the ground around the new green. His face was shining as he carried out his task. With the stakes in place he wove twine around them to keep our dogs from despoiling the new growth.

I stared at my him with keen interest. I didn't want to be sent inside so I sat as quietly as I could while Dad went about his task. Finally I could stand it no longer which must have been about five minutes or a little less. "What are the sticks for?"

He smiled. "This is to keep you and the dogs away from my putting green." He thought for a moment. "The dogs' paws and all your running around will tear up the grass and ruin the putting green. You will keep off the green, won't you, Son?"

I nodded as if I understood, and with most likely a sparkle in my eyes, I asked another question. "What's a putting green for?"

In later years I would recognize the smile which stretched my father's lips at that moment. "It's for me." I've seen the expression of intensity and satisfaction that was on his face that day throughout the years on his face as well as my own as I matured. He grinned as he looked at me. "When you get older you're going to be glad this is here."

He sent me into the house after answering that question. Most likely he didn't want my over-active curiosity to get the better of me. He knew very well how I was in those days and he was wise enough to have guessed that I would have found a way to get through the twine that he strung to keep me out. If memory serves me correctly there were a few times when that twine did not do the job for which he had put it up, as both the dog and I got through.

In the years which followed I watched my father quietly use this green for putting and for the targeting of his chipping skills. I'll grant you that over the years I have enjoyed many afternoons with friends and associates in the fresh air and the sunshine of a number of different golf courses. There have actually been times when I have gone to the driving range with the specific task in mind of practicing. Dad took the concept of practice to a much grander and loftier level. He would come home from the office or the studios, and for hours he would chip golf balls at the green with his nine iron or pitching wedge. I think it helped him work out the kinks from a day of work.

God, he had patience. Each stroke with the club was analyzed and imperfections were corrected. It seems to me that practice might be hitting about one hundred balls at a time; but, I think, he would hit a thousand or more. It was his passion to be the very best that he possibly could be at his chosen avocation. It was a matter of pride for him that his game, and the strokes of the club that comprised it, were as near perfection as possible.

****

There was no doubt that Randolph Scott was a perfectionist and a master of his passion with the game of golf. His sense of the art went much deeper than the technical aspects of the game, too. Golf to him was more than walking around a golf course and hitting a little, white plastic-coated ball into eighteen holes and then saddling up onto a bar stool. The manners and the courtesies of the game were just as important to him as the mechanics of the game. I suppose some of his gracious manner and courtesies came from the Southern way he was raised. The rest of it came from the history and the culture that manifested itself as a gentleman's sport.

Let me give you an example of what I'm trying to explain. The game of golf has a terrifying effect on the greens and fairways of a golf course. Divots are gouged from the well-manicured turf of the fairway with almost every shot. Indentations are beaten into each green with each successful high-arcing chip shot. More often that not there are numbers and legions of golfers who refuse or are unaware that these conditions are their responsibility to correct. If you take a chunk of the fairway out with a shot, I was always taught by my father that courtesy demanded you replace it. If you put a dent in the green, you were supposed to use a golf tee or some other pointed object to smooth it out. Small courtesies such as these make the game better for the players who follow behind.

When I first started playing golf with my father in the early 1960s he would mercilessly drill the courtesies and the manners of the game to me. Each time I took a fairway shot and made a divot without picking it up he would just stand over it. "Chris. Pick up the divot and replace it."

I would shrug and give a heavy sigh. It didn't seem that important to me at that age. Really it seemed a little silly. "Yes, Dad." I would trudge over to the chunk of fairways I had dug up and thrown to the wind. Packing the moist sod onto the brown nakedness of the ground from where it had been ripped, I stepped on it to force it back to its proper level.

My father would smile. He was proud of his beliefs in the game and the necessary tasks that accompanied it. "If every-one did that these fairways would be perfect all the time. It's just good manners to leave the course looking good for the people who will be playing behind us." One time I can easily recall he stood in front of me and explained, "You have to show the proper respect, not just for the next person, but to the game. The people who own these courses spend a great deal of money to keep them in a playable condition. If you want to use the course you have to show it the respect it deserves."

Divots in the fairway were one thing, but the high-arcing chip shots to the green were a real stickler for my father as well. A well-hit chip shot from a few dozen yards from the green can leave a distinct indentation in the green. Dad would very carefully stoop low to the grass, and using a tee or a bent over fork, prod the green back to its original flatness even if it was not his ball which had made the mark. It annoyed him no end if he set up a putt and discovered one of those indentations left by a less courteous golfer.

I can see him lining up his putt with the careful scrutiny of a nuclear scientist. He would be about ready to shoot when he would see it. "Judas Priest! The manners of some of these people!" He would prod the section back to flat and then turn to me. "Do you see why I always tell you to be careful about these greens, Chris?"

I would nod my head in righteous agreement.

Now it seems more or less reasonable to follow those general guidelines. I know that I do every time I play although I don't indulge in the game very often these days. At two separate times my father was put on the green's committee of two separate country clubs. He was on the committee at the

Bel-Air Country Club. I was relatively young at that time so I remember almost nothing of it. I do remember when he was on the Greens Committee of the Eldorado Country Club in Palm Desert. I vaguely recall a few unflattering remarks that passed behind his back about his leadership on the committee. I can see their point as I look back. Dad was a pain in the backside about his insistence that all the members of the club, and their guests as well, do their best to keep the greens and fairways in the best possible shape. That meant that all of the members were required to do their fair share.

It's unfortunate that many of the members felt that they were above such menial tasks as replacing divots. As I said, I understand why many of the people felt that way. I don't agree with them, however. Dad was quite correct in what he wanted them to do, but you just can't convince some people of that. The courtesy eludes far too many of them, and the courtesy was a part of the game to my father. It was his way of paying respect to the traditions and history of the game.

****

It's funny when I think back on it now. Golf wasn't the only passion in my father's life. Everything in his life was approached with the same exuberant enthusiasm and vigor he exuded in his search for perfection in the game of golf. I guess maybe that's why he was so popular in the movies as well. That quality seems to jump out at you from the celluloid film which captured his physical form. Work, play or family. It didn't really seem to matter what the medium. Dad always treated it as if it was special and important. It might have been the reason he was so focused in all that he undertook.

Of course, there are some humorous aspects to his passion and his great intellectual focus. My father loved sports even though no other sport or activity came close to approximating his passion for the game of golf. Still, he loved all sports. Television was just becoming popular as I was growing up. I know that there were many times my sister and I would have to break away from a program to have dinner with my parents. On these occasions we were not allowed to watch television.

My mother and father both considered watching television a luxury that was reserved for special times of the day which would occur after dinner and homework. It would be rude to watch it during dinner or conversational moments with the family.

That, of course, was when I was young. I'm not sure when it changed, but when I was a teenager a television was placed in the lanai. In that room there was a fireplace which I don't recall was ever used. It was high off the floor and had a brick counter or shelf that ran underneath it. As a matter of practicality the television was placed there. It could easily be viewed by anyone in the room in that location. It wasn't to be used by anyone (including the children) during dinner or lunch. We ate together as a family during lunch and dinner. I think it was put there originally for the cook to use during the slack times of the day when we were not using that room. It was just one wall away from the kitchen.

Dad loved football, baseball and golf. It didn't happen very often, but occasionally there would be a golf match on the television, and on rare occasions a football or baseball game on the radio at the same time. I must have been fifteen at the time of this incident, although I'm sure it had happened before that. We sat down as a family for lunch. If memory serves me correctly it was a Sunday. Dad was the first one in the lanai. He had the golf tournament on the television. He watched intently but he also had a small radio up to his ear. I presume it was the baseball game. When lunch was on the table, he put down the radio but he left the television on with the sound turned off. After a few moments he picked up the radio and pressed it to his ear. He might as well not have been in the room. Comments directed to him were ignored. He was into both games big time.

Dad was completely focused on the game. I needed to ask him if he was going to take me to the beach the next day as that afternoon and evening I was going with some of my friends to a movie. "Dad. Dad?"

He didn't respond. The radio he held to his ear was loud enough that I could hear it several feet away. It was also quite obvious that he was not wearing his hearing aid which may have made him more able to hear my voice above that of the announcer.

I tried again to politely gain his attention. "Dad, I was wondering if you would . . . " My voice trailed off as it was not even registering that I was speaking to him. His eyes and ears were obviously too busy.

My mother looked over at him. "Randy." Her voice grew louder. "Randy, you put that radio down right now. Your son wants to ask you a question."

My father looked over at my mother and smiled in compliance. "What is it, Son?" He looked at me as his thumb gently turned the volume control of the radio.

I cleared my throat. "I was wondering if you were going to take me to the beach tomorrow morning before you play golf. Mom said that she would pick me . . . up . . . " Once again my voice trailed off as my father put the small transistor radio to his ear. "Dad, are you going to take me?"

He smiled but I knew he wasn't listening.

Mom was getting a little steamed at Dad's interest in the games. She leaned over to him. "Randy, you're setting a bad example for the children."

He looked over at her with the slightest sheepish smile. "You're right, Pat." His eyes turned to me. "Yes, I would be more than happy to take you to the beach tomorrow."

"Thanks, Dad. I have to go." I left the table to join up with my friends who were waiting for me at one of the houses down the street. I heard my mother chastising him as I left. I just know that Dad's thumb was gradually rolling the volume up as she spoke to him. It wasn't an argument, as they rarely, if ever, argued, but more of an object lecture for my father. It is nice to know that even he had his human failings.

This incident is one of the few times I can remember my mother chastising my father. It's too bad I wasn't thinking well back then, or I might have asked my dad for something outlandish. He might have agreed without ever realizing it. Ah, the pains of being raised with scruples.

****

Watching Randolph Scott films like *Gunfighters, The Walking Hills* or *The Fighting Man of the Plains,* one might never suspect that he indulged himself in the beauty of nature by doing a great deal of the gardening and landscaping of his own home. It wasn't really a guarded secret, but if you were not personally aquainted with him, it is not an obvious characteristic. Gardening and tending the lush vegetation surrounding his home was a quiet way for him to relax in the few leisure times his shooting schedule allowed.

There was another passion in Randolph Scott's life, and I'll bet most of you will not be able to guess what it was. He loved tending the plants which surrounded the house. We had a gardener who came to the house on a weekly basis. Leng, who lived in a small apartment behind the house, was somewhat of a majordomo in our household. On the days when the gardener was not in attendance, Leng was, along with all his other duties to my father and the house, taking care of the plants and the yard. Beyond all of this attention Dad felt it necessary that he, too, should tend to the plants.

Now, we didn't have a garden in the traditional sense, but we had an inordinate number of elephant ears, pampas grass, bamboo and ivy that my dad felt needed almost constant care. The plants lined every walkway and the motor court as well as covered the lines of the roof and overhangs. From the street you could tell that there was a house behind the plants, but the features and distinctions were well obscured by the growth. When the vegetation was first planted it was most likely to add accent and warmth to the lines of the house. I think it grew far better and faster than my father and mother originally planned. As a consequence it required constant trimming and care which Dad loved to do.

If he were home during an afternoon after work or after a round of golf, he would slip into his work clothes. The elephant ears were a special project of his. No one trimmed them or cut them back without my father being close by to inspect. They grew well and reached out to the sun from the tender care they were given. Unfortunately elephant ears have a tendency to be rather top-heavy, and given the cobbled areas where they were, they pushed over the edge. This meant that without supports they most certainly lean down and have a tendency to break or get in the way of cars parking in the court. Any given afternoon during my teenage years would find Randy supporting one or another of these plants. He placed the supports carefully and lovingly attached the drooping plants.

As with his golf he felt that perfection in his vegetation was a matter of practice and diligence. Watching him work tirelessly and lovingly over the plants was fascinating. He was so focused in his chores. There was not a false or non-deliberate motion or action. Nothing seemed to slip by him. Much of the lush vegetation that surrounded our house was like that found in more tropical climes. As a result some of it drooped and grew over and around the walkways of the house. Paths along the side of the house that were intended to be wide with the vegetation used as accent or decoration became narrower and occasionally fouled by the copious growth.

The plants outside suffered through and endured the growing years of children and their friends. Our boundless energy and running outside games were a vexation. We ran around the house with the vitality and indulged vigor strictly reserved for children, and hid among the fronds and leaves. On occasion a frond from the elephant ears would be sacrificed.

There was so much vegetation that when one of those leaves would be damaged or broken off it was hard to fathom that my father would be readily able to notice it. Unfortunately he always did. It didn't matter what time of day it was. If he saw it, he would immediately trim the frond or reattach it so that it wouldn't suffer. He would cast a stern eye at my friends and me. He'd do his best to caution us about the plants, but I think he knew there would have to be casualties until my friends and I got old enough to avoid the hanging vegetation.

We would run from the motor court like wailing Banshees. If my dad was quick enough when I was young he would pull me to one side before the plants in my general vicinity were sacrificed. "Son, you've got to be more careful around the plants. It takes me a great deal of work to keep them looking this way." There was a specific seriousness which etched his face when he tried to explain his point.

I would nod my head and respectfully answer. "Yes, sir. I'm sorry." Then I would run to catch up with my friends with the gentle lesson evaporating with every step. It is a good thing my father was a patient man. I wonder, during those times when I was running around with my friends, if he ever considered slipping a Valium into my milk before I went out to play.

Of course as I grew older and on into my late teens, occasionally I would get drafted into helping him . . . sometimes at really inappropriate times. One time I was walking out to my car to go on a date. I was sixteen years old. It was five thirty in the afternoon. My father was struggling with one of the elephant ear plants that had grown huge over the years. "See you later, Dad. I'll be home late." I opened the car door tossing my jacket into the passenger's seat.

I had just gotten my right foot into the car when my dad called out to me. "Chris, come here and help me for a minute." Judging by the coy smile on his face, he knew that I couldn't refuse his request.

I was dressed up but my father needed help, so I acceded. "Sure, Dad. What do you want me to do?"

"Lift this plant up while I support it with this stake."

I pushed up against the massive bulk of the plant and helped him set the pole or the stake into place. Standing up I realized that I had gotten my clothes dirty. "Have you ever thought of cutting these way back?" To me they had always seemed an annoyance, although I have to say that I liked the look of the vegetation.

My dad smiled impishly and chuckled under his breath. "Son, this is the way they are supposed to be. Just think of this as paying back the plants and your old father for all the trauma you gave us when you were young." He chuckled thinking his comment very funny.

I laughed. "Yeah, well don't let it happen again."

He bowed at the waist with a jovial gleam in his eyes. "Oh, yes sir, I won't ever let it happen again. I'm so sorry for taking you away from your date." My father was most certainly a tease. It was special to me to have those times wandering about us. It was affectionate teasing, and it made me feel very warm when we engaged in it.

Working in the garden usually put him in a great mood. He became amusing and playful on those occasions, or at least he thought he was pretty funny. I left for my date as he watched me drive down the street. Judging by the look on his face as I drove away he was still pretty pleased with his comments.

I have to make one final disclosure in this small section before I continue further. I stated that Dad would change into his work clothes to work on the yard and the plants. Most of us have a set or two of clothes we like to wear around the yard or when we work on our cars or boats. For me those clothes usually include a cut-off shirt, a pair of grubby shorts and a pair of sneakers which, if my mother saw them, would be in the trash can in seconds. Dad, on the other hand, wore a pair of pants and an old golf shirt. He looked better working on the garden than I do on an average night when I'm going out to eat dinner. If it was cold outside the outfit included a button up sweater, usually cashmere, and an ascot. As I said, he usually looked better than I did when I was going out for a casual evening.

I wonder if this goes back to his early days in Hollywood when stars were supposed to present a specific image at all times? It may also have been a habit from his youth. The South has most always been slightly more formal and dignified in its presentation. Whichever—it was the habit remained with him.

****

Daniel Webster defines legend as being "a notable person, or the stories told about that person's exploits." Political legends were the likes of George Washington or Thomas Jefferson. Historical legends numbered Daniel Boone and Davey Crockett. The scientific community boasted Alexander Graham Bell, Albert Einstein and Thomas Edison. Literature held up for acclaim Ernest Hemingway, C. S. Lewis and scores too numerous to mention as authentic legends. By the time Randolph Scott

made his best films he had long established himself as a legend in the motion picture industry with others like John Wayne, Errol Flynn, Clark Gable, Charlie Chaplin and Cary Grant. You only had to mention their names to understand the impact they had on the American people.

They say that practice makes perfect. If that is true, then by 1958 at the age of sixty Randolph Scott was a master. Films like *Thunder over the Plains, Riding Shotgun, The Bounty Hunter, Rage at Dawn, Ten Wanted Men, Tall Man Riding, A Lawless Street* and *Seven Men from Now* would not have to have been good films to enjoy popularity due to Randolph Scott's box office acceptance. Truthfully, the movies were good and getting better. *Seventh Cavalry, The Tall T, Shootout at Medicine Bend, Decision at Sundown* and *Buchanan Rides Alone* are considered classic "Randolph Scott films". Classics because of the effort and dedication of the star to make each film better than the last.

It wasn't until I was much older that I realized just how much practice my father put forth to become as he was. When I was young, it used to irritate me that he was never wrong. Everything he did, whether mental or physical, seemed so effortless. When making films I have heard that his memory of scripts was flawless. He was prepared when he got to the set. In business his keen sense and wise decisions were as near flawless as one can achieve.

It's intimidating when you are young to be near someone like that. As I got older, I finally figured out the whys and the hows of his abilities. His thirst for knowledge was unquenchable. Beyond that, he learned from what knowledge he had already amassed. Mistakes made in the pursuit of a particular goal were analyzed and stored away for reference should the situation arise in the future. He paid attention to detail as he felt that it was the small, seemingly insignificant factors that could play the greatest havoc with his plans and goals. This was his practice. This was how he managed to be so competent. He worked at it with the same thoughtful care and manner that he crafted his golf game. There were no insignificant factors which could be pushed aside in favor of the grander design. Practice and experience had taught him well. All factors of the question or the problem must be figured into an equation before a satisfactory answer or result could be achieved.

I must have driven him crazy as I was growing up. I was too busy looking at the end result to see the wisdom of his insistence about detail. I made a great many mistakes that way. I used to want to be able to do something well the very first time I tried it, even though my father attempted to educate me to the fact that there was a satisfaction and a value to practicing. I never saw my dad fail at anything while I failed so often. As with many children I didn't see the failures my father had to experience along the way. All I saw was this larger-than-life man who moved so easily throughout his life.

Even though I had been tutored by Brian Fay in my teens I was still not very good at mathematics. My dad came into my room one Thursday evening. It had to be a deliberate visitation if you understand where my room is. The way our house was laid out it wasn't possible to just find yourself near my room. My parents' rooms were on one side of the house and my room was on the opposite. You had to walk from one end of the house through the living room and the kitchen to get there. So you can see that coming to see me was definitely an intended excursion. In any event, I had just quit attempting to do my algebra homework. I slid my book forcefully over the surface of my desk as my father walked in.

He raised his eyebrows as he watched the book slide over my desk. "What's the matter?" He picked up the math book and thumbed through the pages.

I turned to look at him. "I just don't understand this math. It seems as if I'll never get the hang of it."

He shook his head slightly. He was doing his best to be empathetic. "Did you ask Brian to help you?" His fingers opened the book and turned a few pages.

"Yes, I did. He showed me but I don't seem to be able to keep it in mind." I was definitely frustrated.

Dad looked at the homework sheet that described the

problems my class was supposed to do for class the next day. "Your teacher doesn't give you all of the problems in the book to do. Why don't you try some of the other problems?" In my youth I didn't appreciate the wisdom of my father's counsel nearly as much as I do at my age now.

I was a teenager and a more or less normal one at that. He just asked me to do more work. I looked at him as though he were crazy. "Dad, I don't have time to do all of those questions. I have other homework too."

Dad smiled. "Did you hit a baseball the first time you swung at it?"

I shook my head.

"Well, mathematics is very much like baseball or any other sport. It's practice that makes the difference between poor and excellent performances. In baseball the more you swing the bat the better the odds are that you will hit the ball. In mathematics the more problems you do the better the chance is that you will be able to do better on other problems."

I had never thought of it that way but it made a kind of sense. It wouldn't be until I took college level physics that I would come to fully appreciate that line of logic, however. Practice. I should have seen it coming before he started talking to me. The logic is, of course, as inescapable as it is valuable.

Make no mistake. Life wasn't always easy for my father. No one handed him anything. There were no give-a-ways in his life. He worked hard for everything he had acquired, and he had aspired to be the best he could be. Herein lies the key to my way of thinking. He was never satisfied with the ordinary or the mundane. I think regardless of what occupation he had chosen that that thought would have been his driving force. He wanted to be the very best he could possibly become — not just as an actor or a business man, but as a father and a husband as well.

In films and in business I don't think he really got a sense of just how good he really was. He was just pursuing his version of perfection is his life. I don't think he ever looked around and truly realized how close he had come to achieving that goal. Even if he had it would not have been enough because he would have examined it to find something more he could have done to improve it. It was not perfection that pushed him, to my way of viewing it. It was the constant looking at his performance and trying to be just a little better the next time.

I wonder if this couldn't in part be the reason he was modest and unassuming in his view of himself? Each role and business decision was just a step on the way to gaining what he most wanted . . . his best effort. I imagine it would be hard to be conceited if you thought you could do better. That translates into drive. This may also be one of the reasons he never succumbed to the hype and the glitz of the industry. Modesty prevented him from thinking he was some big deal. He was just a man doing a job and trying to do it the very best he could. There was no great glory in that but certainly a sense of nobility and pride of one's chosen craft.

Thoreau stated that most men lead lives of quiet desperation. If that is true, then my father was one of the lucky ones. He was constantly striving to be better each day than he was the day before. This is one of the lessons I learned by growing up with him as my father. Failure to him was merely a stepping stone on the path that leads to success. I'm very glad he imparted that lesson to me as it has been of great comfort to me the times I have failed. As a side note: it wasn't until much later in my own life that the logic of this became apparent to me. Once I learned the lessons my father tried so very hard to instill in me, I stopped being desperate and began living with the same passion and inner power that was so evident and well defined in him.

He treated his children the same way. While I'm sure he wanted my sister and me to be the class geniuses, he only wanted to make sure that we did our best regardless of the outcome. He got lucky with my sister. She was the straight-A student. It's a good thing he had a sense of humor about me. I was always the struggling student. My grades were passing but Dad knew in his heart that I was capable of much more.

Still, he only asked me to do the very best I was able and he was genuinely pleased if I did. "Son, I don't care if you are ever an 'A' student as long as a 'C' represents your very best effort. You don't have to be the best at anything to make me proud of you. What you have to do is to try your very best at whatever it is you are doing." He looked at me with such wisdom and understanding. I wish I had seen past my own insecurities when I was younger so that it would have mattered to me.

The first time he said that I looked up at him with a questioning stare. "Really? But what if I fail?"

My father smiled gently. "You can't fail if you do your best. Not everything is going to be your cup of tea. You may not succeed at everything, but it is important that you put forth your very best effort in whatever venture you choose." His eyes were very gentle and understanding as he made that comment.

It made me feel less a failure at the time, but it also sparked in me a drive that would come to full force later in my life. It ignited the intelligence to keep trying if I really wanted to accomplish something.

"Practice, practice, practice." I heard him say that all my life. "If it's worth doing, it's worth doing right." All my life those statements have rung in my ears. It was one of the things my father kept telling me. I have used that philosophy more and more as I have aged. This even relates to projects and jobs which have no real significance to my livelihood. Any effort I participate in I do with the thought in mind of giving it the very best effort of which I am capable.

In watching my father as he set about various projects and endeavors he certainly practiced what he preached. He paid meticulous attention to detail without respect to the nature or the importance of the task. It was not an obsessive or compulsive attention but the kind of attention which patience and logic dictate must be taken if you are to succeed. In this way simple and obvious mistakes are taken out of the equation.

When we are young and our parents try to teach us, it is amazing how much we disregard their words. Sometimes we turn around after we have grown up and we realize how right they were. I know I did. I was simply amazed when I woke up one morning and I heard some of my father's thoughts rolling around in my head. Now they were my thoughts. I guess he really did know what he was talking about after all. As a writer

I know very well how accurate and correct he was when he told me that a job worth doing is a job worth doing right. It may not seem like it sometimes, but I really work at this craft.

****

The last four pictures which starred Randolph Scott were a fitting culmination to a career of excellence and dedication to the craft of acting and the audiences who were so faithful for several decades. *Ride Lonesome, Westbound Comanche Station* and his last film *Ride the High Country,* which featured Randolph Scott's old motion picture friend Joel McCrea. Each one of these films was an excellent motion picture. Since 1962 when *Ride the High Country* was released, there have been no more "Randolph Scott films." Still there are three or four generations who know what a "Randolph Scott film" is. The reason, I think, is that the man took his job and his responsibility to his audience very seriously. He would not settle for anything less than his best. He wouldn't expect his audience to accept anything less than that either. The same was true in his personal life.

Do you do something that if it were taken away from you, you would die? I think my father did. All my life I watched him play golf. As I stated earlier, it was his passion. More so than all the other activities in his life, Dad was a golfer. It was his exercise and his social medium. He didn't like large groups of people but playing a round of golf with three of his friends was just the right number for him. There was unhurried time to chat and talk as they walked the eighteen holes. It was private. My father was nothing if he was not a private man.

When he retired from the motion picture industry and settled into life as a business man, I think golf took on an even greater level of importance. True, it was a social vehicle and a place to discuss business at a leisurely pace, but it was also his refuge. It was where all the passion and the practice was given life and form. The sport was his activity. He shared it with my mother when they were younger and later with me as I grew up, but it was *his* activity. He loved the game and all that went into it.

In the early 1980s when my father began having trouble with his heart, he went through a period of time where he couldn't play his game. The doctors who attended him in Los Angeles and at the Mayo Clinic back East wanted to fit him with a pacemaker that would make his heart work properly. Once that was accomplished he again began playing golf. After a few years, however, he was advised to stop playing. Stop playing?! After he stopped playing for a year he looked terrible to me. He lost weight and his attitude was different. The changes may have been subtle, but to me they were striking. I might not share this ordinarily but there is a point to be made at this particular juncture. His health seemed to deteriorate rapidly after that. It hurt me to see him deteriorate and was even worse to see his once-sparkling eyes dim.

On a few occasions I caught him staring out the living room window at the golfers hitting their drives from the fourth tee of the Los Angeles Country Club which, as I said earlier, was just across the fence from our backyard. On one occasion I sat in the chair just across from his and put a question to him. "Dad, why don't you just go and play a few holes?"

The glimmer that used to light his eyes when he thought about golf in years past wasn't there when he looked at me and gave me his answer. "I can't, Son. The doctors have told me that it's just too hard on my heart. He sighed and turned his eyes toward the men at the fourth tee."

It angered me that age should be so unfair to my father. There was no justice in this. His passion was being taken away from him and there was nothing he could do about it. Golf was the arena where he had spent a great deal of time with my mother, before skin cancer drove her out of the sun, and with me in my youth. So much of his life revolved around the game and the course. It just wasn't fair. "You know you should just forget about what the doctors have told you. Golf is your favorite thing in the world. I'd rather see you die on the course than to see you here just looking out at the course." I was frustrated. It seemed so criminal to me that he should be denied that which he loved so dearly.

He reached over to me and patted my hand. His hand was so frail compared to how it looked when I was younger. "I appreciate what you are saying, Chris, but I have to do as the doctors have instructed me." A little sparkle lit his eyes in response to my concern.

I didn't want him to die foolishly. I did want to see the sparkle that lit his eyes when he came back from playing. Oh, as he got older he complained that he hadn't shot a good round. That was all right as long as the sparkle was still evident in his eyes. I missed that sparkle in the last few years of his life. I would have given anything to have seen it there just one more time before he passed away. I'm not sure if it would have been moral or ethical to have traded a year or two of his life to have seen that glimmer of life and passion in his eyes just that one last time.

As passionate as my father was about golf, I am passionate about sailing. I have worked at it the great majority of my life. Nothing in this world gets into my soul and under my skin as the feel of the wind in my face and the movement of a well-trimmed sailboat beneath my feet. I owe my ability to experience that sort of passion directly to watching my father — the care and the attention to all the details of the mechanics, as well as the meticulous preservation of the courtesies of the rules and the traditions which are an integral part of the sport. It would be difficult in my mind to separate the two.

The look I see in my eyes after a day of sailing is so close to the look I saw in my father's eyes after he played golf that it is almost as frightening as it is inspiring. I learned that lesson very well. I have found that this sense of passion and wonder has invaded all aspects of my life as I am sure it did in his. The single expression of passion is incapable of being held into one tiny corner of your life. It expands until it is a cornerstone of your thinking and your view of life. Passion makes you dissatisfied with anything but a best effort. I remember my father said that if you are doing your best you are always looking for something else you can do to make it better. To this day I, too, am never satisfied with any job I do as I know that

Dad combined both his passions as often as he could.

somewhere in it there is something I could have done to make it better.

In 1976 I bought my first real sailboat. It had taken me many months to refurbish it and to make it into exactly what I wanted. I deposited all the love of life and the love I possessed for the ocean into this boat. It was the first real opening of the door to my passion for sailing, and it flowed through me and washed over me with a sensation I still relish to this day. I couldn't imagine any greater feeling. As was my habit I frequently went to my parents' house to visit even during the time I was restoring the boat. On one visit I was sitting in the living room with my father. We were both sipping a beer. I knew that he had been playing golf so I decided to ask him a question that popped into my mind. "Dad, is there anything in this life which you would give up for golf?"

A curious smile crossed my father's lips and shook his head. I can only imagine what images I conjured in his head as I looked at his smile.

I rephrased the question. "If you had to give up either golf or sex, which one would you give up?" I really wanted to hear his answer, even though I was half-heartedly teasing with him.

He looked me straight in the eyes and smiled. "If I had to choose I would probably give up sex," his eyes glimmering with impish delight as he answered. "But fortunately I don't have to choose." He fancied his answer quite comical as he chuckled. He really did look very cute and smug as he sat back in his well-used yellow chair. Anytime he could get away with answering a question in that manner it pleased him.

The practice and the effort to achieve and accomplish are the extensions of passion. You cannot pursue perfection if you do not hone your skills or put forth a best effort. You cannot have learned if you are not constantly looking for ways to improve and change in your attempt at reaching the level of personal best. I am not as good as a sailor as my father was as a golfer, but then I haven't been working at it as long as he had.

The only thing I pray for is that when I get older I will not have to face the possibility that I will have to give up the one activity which makes my life worth living — sailing. I'm sure it crushed my father when he was told by his doctor that his health would be in jeopardy if he were to continue playing golf. It crushed me to have heard that news. I watched him too many times over the years. I saw what his participation in the game did for him. It gave him life. It made him younger for having gone and played. When it was gone, he changed. His body positioning shifted. His focus of life was altered drastically and it showed in his face. To me it seemed like the spark that kept him younger than his peers extinguished, taking with it the immense will and energy he needed. He aged rapidly after just a short time away from the sport he loved.

I think he saw the passion I held inside for sailing. He encouraged it. I think he saw that as my best course to affect the rest of my life. In his failing health in the early 1980s he came down to see a boat which I had just recently purchased. (No, not a new, high-tech expensive boat. It was a used Islander Bahama 30 — not a bad vessel but not a fancy racing yacht. I couldn't afford things like that.) It took a lot out of him to come down to the boat, but I could tell by the look in his eyes that he appreciated my sense of passion in this newly-acquired vessel. I felt sorry for the poor yacht broker who sold me the boat because he almost fell over himself when he saw my father was on the dock where he kept some of his brokerage boats. That poor guy went through seven kinds of heart failure keeping the other brokers and customers away from my boat. My dad didn't want any fanfare connected with his visit, but he was prepared to endure it just so he could see my boat. That simple act made me feel validated in my father's eyes.

I know in the past few years, as my writing has become more accepted and I have worked harder at perfecting it, that I have had little time to sail. It is enough for me to know that my boat is a few miles from my house. It is enough to know that if I want to I can turn off my computer for the day and spend a few hours indulging in my passion. If that were taken away from me I think I, too, would pass away rapidly. On the other hand if my boat was just outside my window and I knew I couldn't sail it ever again, it would at the very least cripple me. I have wondered in the years since my father's death if that wasn't true about him living next to the golf course. Did he look out longingly at the people playing the sport he was denied, and did it eat away at him? Or did it bring him some comfort knowing that it was right there beyond the fence that was around our yard? I guess I'll never know but it does give me pause to reflect and wonder from time to time.

Looking back I wish I had persuaded my father to have taken the time to go sailing with me. I think he would have enjoyed it. It never occurred to me when I was young, but I think he would have liked the idea that his passion heavily influenced my passion. I still practice all the lessons which he did in adhering to the tradition and style of my sport. There are no divots on the ocean to be replaced, but there is the traditional and historic courtesy which yachtsmen give to one another. I do it out of respect to my passion and out of love to the man who taught me.

Chapter 4

HUMOR

There is a scene in *Decision at Sundown* where Andrew Duggan as the sheriff of the town is trying to intimidate Randolph Scott's character, an out-of-town stranger. The scene takes place in a saloon. The sheriff takes the stranger's money and drops it in a spittoon. With a sly smile on his face, Randolph Scott leans over and picks up the cuspidor, placing it gently on the bar between Andrew Duggan and him. A twinkle of impishness dances in Randolph Scott's eyes, and a mischievous smile crosses his lips. He looks the sheriff in the eye and says to him, "Sheriff, I'd sure appreciate it if you'd get my money out of there, wipe it off and put it back on the bar."

Without seeing the action of the picture, a sense of the humor is lost, but it is there all the same. Humor in most Randolph Scott films was subtle and served often to emphasize the seriousness and determination of the character. There were some films, however, like *Home Sweet Homicide*, *Rebecca of Sunnybrook Farm* and *Susannah of the Mounties*, where the humor was much more obvious and intentional. In his films — as in his personal life — the smiles and the humor came honestly and genuinely.

I know my dad had a good sense of humor. For one thing he had to, having had me as a son. This is in itself more or less proof positive that he had at least a subtle sense of the ironic. There are some other indicators that Randolph Scott had a well-developed sense of humor. He had a very dry and wry way of expressing himself. There were times when his eyes would light up and a thin devilish or impish smile would creep up onto his face. No one in the family was safe at those times and his friends might be in even greater jeopardy. He was also a consummate tease. I should know because on many occasions I was the target of his mischievous attitude. It's just as I described the day that I heard the Statler Brothers' song about my father. It tickled him to be one jump ahead of me, and unfortunately he was frequently one jump or more ahead.

****

My father loved going to Dodger baseball games. So much so that his reserved season tickets placed him in the first row of the bottom level halfway between home plate and first base. The two seats directly behind belonged to Fred Astaire. He and Fred were long time friends and they spent a great deal of time together. It seemed to me that Fred liked joking around with my father almost as much as he liked joking around with Fred. Now the jokes were not obvious as you might think. They revolved around subtlety.

I remember one occasion very well. I was sixteen years old. In the days before I discovered it was bad for my back, I was given possession of my father's 1955 T-Bird. On one particular Saturday I was in the motor court waxing my car for a date I had that night. I looked up when I heard the roar of a car turning the corner and speeding down the dead-end street where our house is. It was a black T-Bird much like the one I was waxing. It belonged to Fred Astaire. He and Dad were going to go the baseball game at Dodger Stadium.

Fred had just turned off the motor and was getting out of his car when my dad threw open the front door. He walked out into the motor court and began chastising me about driving down the street so fast. "Christopher! What have I told you about

Fred Astaire was one of Randolph Scott's oldest friends.

driving that fast down the street? There are children in this neighborhood. You would feel terrible if you hit one of them."

I smiled and pointed to the other side of the court to Fred.

Dad looked over and abruptly stopped scolding me. "I'm sorry, Son. It just sounded like your car."

I shook my head. "That's all right. It's nice to know that I'm not the only one who drives that way. Nice to see you, Uncle Fred. I hope you have a good time at the game." I turned away from the two men and went back to waxing my car.

Dad glared at him a little. "Fred, you're setting a bad example for the boy. I keep telling him to slow down coming down this street." He walked over to Fred shaking his head as he approached. They were a funny combination. My father was tall and well built while Fred was much shorter and very slightly built.

Fred smiled warmly. "Sorry, Randy. I was just enjoying the day. I hope I'm not too late?"

My father shook his head at Fred and they walked into the house together.

It was hot that day on the black-surfaced motor court so after a few more minutes I decided to get a cold drink and chat with my father and his friend before they left to go to the game. I liked talking to the two of them. They were like a comedy team only the jokes and the expressions were very subtle.

When Fred Astaire arrived, I hadn't really looked very closely at him. He used to come by the house frequently so there was no real reason to pay that much attention. He did look a little . . . shall we say odd . . . that day. As I walked into the living room, I took a better look at him. Fred had been losing his hair for a number of years so he took to wearing what I always thought were good-looking toupees. This one was different. It made him look a little flamboyant — you might even say a little on the gay side. Maybe effeminate would be a better choice of terms, but somehow I doubt it.

Dad seemed not to notice how odd Fred looked. Knowing my father, I would have expected him to have made a comment to Fred, but he didn't. Fred made no mention of it so the two men left in my father's car. Many hours later the two men came back to the house. Dad offered Fred a drink. He opened a

Coors for himself and the two men sat in the solarium that is just outside my father's room and talked. I was just getting ready to leave for my date. I went to say good-bye to my father and to pay my respects to Mr. Astaire. I couldn't help but stare at Fred Astaire when I stood in front of him to shake his hand.

Fred chuckled a little and looked over at my dad. "By the way, Randy, what do you think of my new hair piece?"

My father smiled askance at Fred.

"You don't think it's a little odd?" Fred smiled, trying to force him to admit that it looked a little funny.

Dad shook his head. "Well Fred, I was going to mention it earlier but I decided it was better not to say anything." His face was very straight and his voice gave no hint that he meant anything else.

"Well, Randy, this was supposed to have been a joke. You were supposed to have noticed so that I could put a different one on. When you didn't mention anything, I just left it on. Why didn't you say something about the way it looked?" Fred was a little embarrassed having worn that hair piece to the game. He didn't say that, but if the look on his face was any indicator, he was.

Dad shrugged and smiled slightly. "I'm sorry, Fred. I just didn't want to hurt your feelings by telling you how bad that hair piece looked." That twinkle sparkled in Dad's eyes as he spoke. He had known it was a joke all along but had wanted to see how long it would take his friend to say something about it. As a consequence, Fred had worn the joke toupee for the whole day. I could see in my father's eyes that he had loved every minute of it. (I watched *Susannah of the Mounties* just a short while ago and it got me to thinking that a very similar incident was played out in that film by my father. He could have been thinking back to that when this incident happened.)

****

I wondered about my father from time to time as I watched him in his daily routines. He was a very proper and dignified man in most instances, but there were occasions where he took me by surprise by doing something which at the time I considered totally out of character. Not in a bad or negative sense — as it might sound — but as a six-foot-plus man, he at times seemed impish in his wry joviality and style.

One really funny incident comes to mind immediately. I was about eleven or twelve years old. My father and Fred Astaire had invited me and my friend John Stafford to go to the Dodgers game with them. Thoughtful as always, Dad let John and me have the two seats over the opposing team's bull pen, while Fred and he sat behind us.

It was a great game. Dad and Fred were fun as they usually were at the games. You never had to worry about getting enough to eat and drink at the game with those two sitting behind you. They laughed and joked through the whole game even though John and I hardly paid any attention. At the seventh inning stretch Dad stood and asked us how we liked the game. We had been standing for only a few moments when a young girl walked up to my father with an autograph book and a pen clutched tightly in her hand. She couldn't have been more than five or six years old. Her parents must have wanted Dad's autograph but might have been a little embarrassed about asking him directly themselves. I think this is the most logical explanation, because I can't see a girl her age doing this on her own. (You know, I could have been wrong. I have encountered a number of people in their sixties and seventies who have told me "I remember your father when I was just a little child." At the same time I know a large number of people under twenty-one who have made similar statements. I guess the old guy still has appeal.)

The little blonde-haired girl walked up to Dad very nervously. She looked up to him as she stood before him. Hands slightly trembling she asked, "Are you somebody famous?"

My father smiled down at her. His steely eyes sparkled as they always did when he was going to be cute or funny. He stooped a little and bent his knees so that he would be a little closer to the girl. "Yes," he said. "I'm Lassie." A big smile formed on his lips as he spoke. He was just trying to be cute.

The little girl's bottom lip jutted out and the tears welled up in her eyes. She started crying.

My dad knelt in front of her and tried to quiet her. "I'm sorry, honey. I was just teasing." First he handed the little girl his handkerchief and then he took her autograph book. Hurriedly he signed it for her hoping that would stop her flowing tears. He handed it back to her. "I'm sorry, little one. I was just teasing."

While all this was happening John and I were yelling playfully at my dad. "Boy, what a bully. You're making the little girl cry."

Fred, on the other hand, was just smiling boyishly next to my father.

She stopped crying as she looked at the chicken scratch that represented my dad's signature. She smiled as the tears ceased flowing. She stared at the signature and then looked back up at my father. "My father thought you were Gary Cooper," she whimpered. With a heavy sigh she started back up the steps and to whomever had sent her to get the auto-graph. I have a feeling they were close by and were getting as big a laugh as the rest of us.

Fred, John and I laughed so hard I thought I was going to cry.

Dad looked dumbfounded as the little girl walked away. He shrugged his shoulders and smiled sheepishly at John and me.

Fred jabbed Randy in the ribs. He loved it and he wasn't about to let the moment pass without just a little needling. "Well Randy, that will teach you to smart off to a child."

Dad just smiled. "Just watch the game, Fred. Just watch the game."

Fred smiled widely. "I can't imagine why, when it's so much more fun to watch you."

My father chuckled as he sat down in his seat. That's one thing I admired about him. He could take a joke at least as well as he could pass them out. I know that looking back it was a lesson that took a great deal of time for me to learn. Fortunately I had a good teacher.

****

I have always loved how fathers dance with their little girls. My dad was no exception. The only difference between him and many other fathers was the distance vertically between my sister and him. Boy, his legs were long. For him to get down to my sister's level he had to bend his knees and back quite dramatically. It amused me to watch them. It amused me far more when I realized that my sister was not the first little girl with whom he had done this.

I loved watching old movies. I like my father's films but I also enjoyed many of the other films from his era. Although, if I knew one of Dad's films was going to be on, I made special allocation to watch it. He made so many films that it is hard to remember all the ones he was in. You have to remember that, by the time I was old enough to know who my father really was, he had been in the top-ten actors for better than twenty years. I'm still amazed at the number of films which I haven't seen or heard of before.

When I was a teenager in the mid 1960s they showed a great number of his films on television on Saturday afternoons. In those days I was home from surfing about the time they started and I plead guilty that I occasionally had to take a break from the day and watch them. It was an unusual treat to see your father on the screen. I'm glad they still play his old films. It's like a piece of him is still with me. So often when I am writing I leave the television on for background noise. Even if one of my father's movies is playing, I won't watch it as much as listen to snippets as my concentration on my book rises and falls. Hearing his voice is comforting and it really is like having him back, even if it is only for a moment.

The fun part of watching your own father's films was that if you talked to him afterward he would always say something just like he did in the film. I loved that. I think he got a kick out of it as well.

I watched a movie of Dad's called *To the Shores of Tripoli* one Saturday afternoon when I was fourteen. One of the lines in the film was, "I know you can do it, Chris." A little later that day I was talking to my dad about a project that was due in one of my classes at school. He looked down at me. "I know you can do it, Chris." It sounded just like when he said it in the movie. It was perfect. The voice and the inflection were identical as was the look in his eyes.

I was overjoyed and I couldn't restrain the laughter which

forced its way from my belly. "That's great, Dad." Sometimes it is the simple pleasures that make you feel really good.

My father looked at me with an incredulous expression. "What's so funny?" He scratched his head watching me laugh.

I handed him the *TV Guide* and pointed at the name of his film.

He looked at it for a minute and then smiled. "You think that's pretty funny, don't you?" His face was brilliant with his smile. He sat down in his over-stuffed chair.

I nodded my head.

A scampish smile crossed his lips and his eyes twinkled. Here it comes. He was going to zing me. That look was just the forerunner. "Do you remember what happened to the Chris in that film when he didn't do it right?" He winked at me.

I gulped and nodded. He had managed to do it to me again. I was never going to get the better of him, but I was going to try.

His smile twisted to a more devilish expression. "Then you better get to work on that project. Attention! About face! Now get to work." He laughed as I walked away. It just tickled him to turn the tables on me when I was trying to tease him.

There is one point I should interject here. I don't believe my father acted very often. I personally believe that he chose roles that were close in character to his own; as a consequence, it was more like playing himself. That's not acting to my way of thinking. It is more like being yourself on cue. Anyway a friend of mine had said that one of his films was coming on this Saturday. I sat down after taking a shower to wash away the salt and the sand from my morning of surfing and turned on the television.

Much to my surprise there was a Shirley Temple movie playing, *Susannah of the Mounties*. I was disappointed that it wasn't one of my father's films but I left the movie on anyway. I didn't pay much attention to the film as I busied myself with some homework until I heard Shirley Temple's character tell the adult lead in the film that she would teach him to dance. This kind of thing amuses me so I looked up at the screen. The adult male lead was a good-looking man with a moustache. When they started to dance, I almost fell backwards out of my chair. I got closer to the set and strained my eyes to look at the actor who was dancing with Shirley Temple. It was my father in that film! I think he looked pretty good with a moustache but he never wore one in the time since I was born. I can't believe that I didn't recognize him in the beginning. Of course, if I had read the credits I might have seen his name just under Shirley Temple's.

I dashed through the house to talk to him. He got quite a laugh out of my surprise. He never made much comment to us kids about his films or the people with whom he worked. This film had been made before either my sister or I were born. It made him laugh to see my surprise but I think he had to have had quite a good sense of humor to have done the film with her. After all, it is said that you should never act with kids or dogs, as they might upstage you.

****

Being overtly funny or humorous is not the only way to express one's sense of humor. It can be exerted in many ways that may not always be immediately apparent. My sister and I were sometimes the brunt of his subtle humor, but then again he had to put up with the two of us for a great number of years. It seems to me for that you have to have a really good sense of humor.

When I was just fifteen years old and my sister was twelve (actually she was close to thirteen but that isn't important) we decided (or maybe I decided and she just had to be part of it) to take my father's silver 1955 T-Bird out for a drive. Dad had been teaching me to drive for a number of years so I felt quite confident. The trick was to get a key made so that we could pull this stunt off in the middle of the night.

Our house was never designed to keep the kids out of closets or rooms, so careful not to arouse suspicion, I got a hold of a spare key from the kitchen. I couldn't very well ask my mother or my father to take me to the locksmith so I walked down into Beverly Hills to get a duplicate key made. I looked older than fifteen so the locksmith never questioned my need for a new key. The duplicate key had to be made in order for the deception to be unnoticed by either the household staff or by my parents. If the key was missing from the kitchen it would be all over.

In any event I put the original key back in its place. No one was (or appeared to be) the wiser. I showed the key to my sister and we decided to leave in the car the next night. Boy were we clever! Not really very smart looking back but we were certainly clever. About midnight I pushed the car out of the motor court so it could be started without my father hearing it. His bedroom window was just off the court so we had to be at least a short distance away from the house or he would hear us. That meant that I had to get the car up the slight hill of the driveway and into the street. It is a good thing I was as strong as I was tall.

We drove around Beverly Hills and Bel Air for more than an hour and had a great time. At the time I had no idea that the tires on the little car were in dire need of replacement. When we were done we let the car coast into the driveway and into the motor court with the engine and the lights shut off. The next day neither of my parents said anything about our escapade of the previous night. We were feeling pretty cocky about the whole thing since we seemed to have gotten away with our deception. (Now, just so you know, this is where I used to get into most of my trouble as a youngster. As I have found out the hard way, things are rarely as they seem and cockiness is something to be avoided at all costs unless you are really sure you deserve to feel that way.) In hushed tones my sister and I talked about doing it again. We decided as long as we had gotten away with it once, we would do it again that night.

It was a good idea at the time but as I look back on those days, I should never have tried to push my luck. (I think most people learn rather quickly in life that just because you get away with something once doesn't mean that you weren't discovered. Doing it a second time or more usually leads to disaster.) My father's sense of justice and humor was better than mine. As we had the previous night, we again snuck out of the house about midnight. As I had done before, I pushed the car out of the motor court. We both hopped into the car. We were excited. I turned the key. The starter turned but the car wouldn't start. I was frantic and I tried for more than five minutes. The car still wouldn't start. I must have run the car out of gas the day before. No one was coming out to investigate, so I pushed the car back into the drive and put it away. My sister and I were just getting ready to sneak back into the house when I saw my dad standing by the front door. He was just casually leaning against one of the pillars that holds up the roof of the carport and the entry to the house.

We were caught as red-handed as you can possibly imagine. I looked up at my father and started to explain but he stopped me by shaking his head. I walked closer ready to take my punishment.

When I was standing in front of him, I saw that he had the rotor from the distributor in his hand. His eyes were dark and flashing with anger. He reached out his empty hand to me. "Give me the key, Christopher." He didn't yell. That's not too unusual. My father was not one of those parents who ever raised his voice all that much. There was a dark seething anger below his voice which was justified considering what my sister and I had just done.

I handed him the key and looked into his eyes. I just knew I was going to be punished big time. It might have been different if we had been found out but this was worse. We were discovered in the act of doing something that most parents would consider a capital offense.

He looked at me as I stood nervously in front of him in the moonlit motor court. "Go to your room, Chris. We'll discuss this tomorrow." My father's face reflects his moods very well — a little too well at this moment to have suited my fancy.

I was flabbergasted. He didn't yell. He didn't even get angry. Maybe that was the scariest part of the whole incident. As I look back, if that had been me, I would have sworn a blue streak, yelled for a good half an hour and grounded my son for the rest of his life. It's a good thing it wasn't my son. It wasn't my father's way to show his anger and displeasure that way. I walked away from him in silence. Little did I know what he had in store for me the next day.

The next day at breakfast nothing was said to either my sister or me about the car incident. Both of us went to school as usual. It struck me as odd that my father had not said anything. Surely he must have some punishment in mind considering what my sister and I had done. When I got home, I went to my room and started doing homework — that was rare for me, but I didn't want to push my luck any further than I had the night before. Every noise outside my door caused me to jerk up as I knew that my father would be in to talk to me about taking the car.

About an hour after I had gotten home, he came to my room. He was very cool and business-like when he spoke to me. "Son, there is a police detective here to see you. Would you please come into the living room?" He left the room without so much as a backward glance. I don't know how he did it. I would have been furious if a policeman had shown up to speak to my son.

My heart sank into the floor as I walked through the kitchen and toward the living room. I felt like a condemned prisoner taking the walk to the electric chair. A policeman was there to see me and he was a detective. I was in trouble now. Oh my God! I was a criminal! Did my father tell the police what I had done? I didn't know the law very well at the age of fifteen and I wondered if he was going to take me to jail. I walked into the living room with my head hung down. Through fear-clouded eyes I saw a large man in a dark suit sitting on the couch with my parents.

The policeman walked up to me. "Mr. Scott. I just want you to know that one of our cars followed you the other night. I also want you to know how serious it is to be driving a car without a license. The department could keep you from getting a license at all, but considering who your father is, I'm just going to give you a warning." The man looked very serious about what he was saying.

There, of course, was more to the police detective's oration but the passage of time has eliminated all but a few of his thoughts. Suffice it to say that it scared me to death. Years and years later I found out that it was my father who had asked the policeman to come over and give me that speech. I'm sure my dad felt it would have a much more significant impact on me than his grounding me. Well, it did. As I discovered later he was absolutely tickled about his deviousness. I'm not sure how he contained his laughter at the time it was happening.

Actually he wanted to drive home a very specific point which he did far more dramatically than if he had yelled and grounded me. He also meant to insure that I would never again do something like that. I really learned my lesson which was what my father intended. I still think he got a chuckle out of it in his later years if he thought back to it.

Still, it proved once again that I could never get away with anything when it came to my father. He made his point without yelling or demeaning either my sister or me even though I am sure there were times when he would have liked to yell. With or without humor his lessons ultimately had the desired effect on me and, I presume, my sister as well.

****

As parents go I was pretty lucky. If I had to choose a family I think I would have chosen the one with which I grew up. Our family never wanted for very much. Most often my father tried to give us almost everything we wanted, but there were limits. Still, there were occasions when my dad was a little bit on the extravagant side. Sometimes it even amazed me how he knew just what I wanted. I don't think he spoiled us, but he did get a charge out of indulging my sister and me when we were least expecting it.

When I turned sixteen, I inherited Dad's 1955 T- Bird. It's not that I couldn't have gotten a new car; it's just that the T-Bird was a great car. What kid wouldn't appreciate a convertible, hard top, two seater? Since my birthday is in the summer, I don't think I had the top on more than a few times. That isn't exactly what my father wanted me to do, however. He told me to leave the hard top on the car. This was flatly unacceptable to me but I was in no position to argue. There was a way around that problem. When I left the house I would deposit the top at one of my friend's house. That seemed to work pretty well so I thought I could leave the top at the house if my father wasn't home.

One day about two months after he had given me permission to use the car as my own, I left the top of the car at the house. I figured I would be back in time to replace the top before my father found out. It seemed to have worked pretty well. When I got home I didn't see Dad's car at the house so I parked my car and began struggling with the hard top. I had almost lifted it into place when someone spoke to me.

"That looks pretty heavy. Would you like some help?" I spun around almost dropping the top. "Dad, where's your car?" I felt stupid asking that question.

"It's in the garage." He smiled and walked over to the car. He helped me lift the bulky hard top into place. "I didn't think you could do this without great difficulty. That's why I told you to leave the top on." He winked at me. "I always had trouble using the soft top. Have you been able to put it up?"

I nodded. "Yeah, I got it up. Two weeks ago when it rained Robb and I put it up. It was really tight."

He chuckled, as he had owned that car since it was new. "It ought to be tight. That top has never been up before. I could never get it to fit." He leaned over the car a little. He raised his eyebrows as he looked at me. He no doubt wanted to make a point to me. "Next time come to me and we'll talk about changing my mind. Not everything is carved in stone but I have my reasons for asking certain things of you. This time I understand. Let's not have a next time."

"Yes, sir. Thanks for helping me with the top. Next time I'll leave it in the garage." I went to my room to get ready for a date.

It wasn't until winter came along that I found out the one drawback to having such a small car. I also found out why my father rarely drove that car and was so eager to let me have it.

I am six-foot-three inches tall and my father was a little over six-foot-four. Guess what? In the fifties they didn't design cars to fit people that size, at least not in the smaller models like the T-Bird. After a few months with the top up, I started having lower back pain. I told my father and he nodded his head and smiled. He, too, had had the same experience when he drove that car. Neither of us could manage to sit up straight in that car. As tall as we were, we had to kind of hunch over the wheel. This may be OK for short trips but if you are in the car for more than twenty minutes, it can be a painful experience. It's too bad really because a 1955 convertible T-Bird is a cool car. If I still had it, it would be worth a sizable piece of change.

My grades weren't all that good at the time so I was stuck with the T-Bird for the time being. My dad said if my grades improved he would see about getting me a different car for my birthday. Well, my grades were passing by the end of the year. One small glitch, however. The school I had been attending for high school was going to be closing down. My parents thought it to be a good idea if I attended summer school and take a creative writing class at a school in Carmel in Northern California. Part of the reason was they thought I needed some extra help in my writing skills and the other was they wanted me to see how I liked the school. This was in case they decided to send me there for my senior year. (With the luck of the Irish on my side they sent me to a military school in Carlsbad, California, which was right on the beach. Good thing, too. There I was able to surf and I met one of my life-long friends as well.)

The school was good and the class was exceptional, but the month that I spent there couldn't have been over fast enough to suit me. A lot of waves had crashed on the beaches where I surfed in Southern California and I had been stuck up North. One of the teachers at the school offered to drive me to the airport the day I was supposed to leave. I liked this man although I can't remember his name for the life of me. He drove a 1956 Porsche. I always liked Porsches. When I was seven years old I saw one while my dad and I were driving to the store. I pointed to the round little car and turned to my father. "That's the car I want when I get old enough to drive."

He looked crookedly at me. "Christopher, by the time you get old enough to drive there will be a great number of cars for you to choose from that will be much more appealing than that one." He smiled and continued driving. He was commonly looking into the future and seeing it very clearly. He had a way of seeing trends and extrapolating his ideas from that information.

I turned my head as the Porsche whizzed past us and then I looked back at my father. "No, that's the car that I'm going to want." I knew my mind and time has shown that I knew it very well.

Well, he was right about part of what he said. There were a great variety of cars to choose from when I was old enough to drive, but I was still hooked on those round-bodied Porsches. I came close to following the crowd in my choice but my original one held sway.

In any event the teacher and I drove through the gate that forms the entrance to the school and he turned to me and asked me if I would like a turn driving his car. Great question. That's like asking the Pope if he would like to be Catholic. We traded sides. I sat behind the wheel and stared for a few pregnant moments at the controls. I had driven a stick shift only a few times before, so the first few shifts were a little on the rough side. Once I got into the swing of shifting it was an exhilarating experience. It didn't last very long because we were at the airport all too soon.

I said my good-byes and boarded the plane. On the hour or so trip back to Los Angeles, I realized how odd it had been for this teacher to have let me drive his car. My thought processes in those days weren't geared for deep contemplation so I passed it off as a friendly gesture by a thoughtful teacher to a departing student. Besides, I was anxious to get home and see my friends, so solving problems was far from the priority in my mind.

When I arrived at the Los Angeles Airport, my friend Eric Von Stroheim was waiting. He told me that my father had asked him to pick me up. We grabbed my gear from the luggage turnstile and headed to the parking lot. I was squinting to find Eric's little off-white Porsche Speedster. Instead of that car he walked up to a bright red 1965 Porsche. He said he had borrowed it from a friend because his was in the shop. I didn't think about it as I was just glad to be home. It took about forty-five minutes to drive from the airport to the house.

The whole way to my house Eric kept making comments about the car. "This is a great car, isn't it, Chris?"

"Yeah, it's even nicer than yours. Who did you borrow this from?" I looked at him strangely since Eric was a few years older than me and he had owned a Porsche for at least two or three years.

"I borrowed it from Mr. Hightower." Eric was grinning from ear to ear.

I knew the man to whom he was referring. His son, Eric and

I were friends. Mr. Hightower shared Eric's love for Porsches and owned a few of them. Still, it was strange that Eric was speaking of the car in such a strange manner. I just chalked it up to him having one of those days and I was too relieved to be home.

When we got to the house, Eric and I unloaded my things out of the car. I wanted to go see some of my friends whom I hadn't seen in over a month but I needed to spend a little time with my parents. Part of that was out of respect to my parents and the other part was that I really liked talking to them.

Eric and I chatted with my mother and father for almost an hour and then I begged off. "Listen, folks. As much as I want to spend more time with you, I've been gone for several weeks and I would like to go and visit some of my other friends." I got up and motioned for Eric to come with me.

Dad smiled slyly and walked with us to the door. "Now, you drive carefully, Christopher, and don't stay out too late. There will be plenty of time for you to spend with your friends. He leaned against the heavy wooden front door and watched me as I began to walk to the garage.

I started to walk to the door of the garage but I noticed that Eric and my father had stopped at the front door. I turned around and the two of them were smiling like the cat who ate the canary. "What's the problem?"

Eric smiled and my father laughed.

Eric threw me the keys which he had taken from the red Porsche that we had driven from the airport.

I caught them and stared at him questioningly. "What are these for?" I guess I was a little bit slow that night. It never occurred to me that Eric would let me drive his car.

He laughed as did my father. My dad looked at me and asked, "Don't you want to drive your new car?". He laughed so hard.

No wonder Eric was talking so much about that car . . . it was mine. I never will forget that incident. Dad always did like to pull off little stunts like that. I might have been mad under other circumstances that they had pulled a stunt like that, but I don't think so. The reason that my father had stooped to such elaborate subterfuge was partly because he knew I was new to a stick shift and mainly because he liked being clever.

****

Because my father's sense of humor tended to be very dry, much of the joking that went on between his friends and him escaped me. Not all of the time, however. There was one time I remember very well. I must have been close to eight or nine. I was old enough then to go every Sunday to the Episcopal church with my father. I'm not sure how the conversation came up, but he was talking to me about nicknames or personal names we get used to using for our close friends. I think that was about the time my sister started calling me "Cal".

Dad smiled and that twinkle sparkled in his eyes as he spoke. Anyone who has watched some of the old movies which come on all the time, thanks to cable and Ted Turner, knows that Dad's good friend Fred Astaire and Gene Kelly were the two best dancers of the golden age of film. Quite tickled with himself for disclosing it, my father told me that his in-fun name for Fred (My sister and I always referred to him as Uncle Fred in those days.) was "Twinkle Toes".

I thought that was the funniest thing I had heard at that time. Uncle Fred was a shy man. He avoided grand entrances in his daily life. He was far too humble and retiring for that kind of attention getting. He, too, occasionally attended the same church where my father and I went. I think he usually attended a later service which was why we saw him infrequently at the service we attended. About a week after my father had told me Uncle Fred's fun name, we went to church. As we were parking the car, Fred was getting out of his car a short distance away.

As we walked up to the church, I spotted Uncle Fred just entering the doors that led to the main chapel. Even at that age I had a loud voice and I shouted at the top of my lungs, "Hey, Uncle Twinkle Toes, wait for us."

He ditched into the church rapidly as all eyes turned to look for whom I was yelling.

My father laughed. "Christopher, It's not polite to yell that name in public." It was all he could do to contain the laughter. I'm sure he had some explaining to do the next time Fred and he got together.

****

In the 1950s a television show named "Topper" was very popular. One of the lead characters in that show was played by a friend of my father's named Bob Sterling. I don't think their friendship was very close because we only saw him at the house a few times. On one occasion when I was only four or five years old, I got the chance to talk to him. Now in those days kids were far less sophisticated than most of the children I have met in the 1990s. The magic of film and television was more real and genuine. It mystified all of the kids I knew back in those days. Now all the magic is explained by the magicians themselves and even the youngest viewers seem to have knowledge of the technical wonders to be accomplished on film or video.

I walked into my father's room. (I really liked that room. The ceiling was very high. The wall next to my father's bed was all bookcase and cabinets. Even though it was darker than the rest of the house, it had a very warm feeling to it.) Bob Sterling and he were engrossed in a conversation which at my age I could not even begin to fathom. Being as polite as was expected of me in those days, I waited patiently for the two men to finish their conversation. I looked up at Bob Sterling. "Hi, Mr. Sterling. Hi, Dad. Mr. Sterling how do you make yourself invisible on the television show?"

Bob Sterling laughed.

I didn't understand the humor of my comment but it didn't discourage me from continuing. I looked up at him very seriously. "Can you do it for me now?"

I thought my father was going to bust a gut he was laughing so hard.

Bob Sterling was a little kinder to my feelings, as he tried to hide the chuckles that were turning his face red.

I didn't understand what was so funny at the time. I had asked what I thought to be a very serious question about something I had seen just a few nights ago on the tube.

It was obvious that my father wasn't taking my comments

very seriously.

Fortunately Bob Sterling was more cautious about my question than my father was, although I'm sure it was taking a lot of self control, as I look back, for him to keep from laughing out loud at my question.

My dad grinned widely at Bob and chided him to explain the disappearing stunt he managed on the show. "Come on, Bob. Tell the boy how you do that disappearing stunt on your show." Dad thought he was being pretty cute at that moment, as evidenced by the chuckle hidden beneath his words.

Bob thought for a few moments. Taking a deep breath he began explaining. "Well, Chris. They have a very special pill that we take that makes us disappear."

Incredulously I stared up at him. "Really?! Can you give me some of those pills?"

This set my father off into another laughing jag. He and Bob looked at each other.

I can still see this quite clearly in my mind. I'm sure that Bob Sterling was thinking what he could do to get back at my father for putting him on the spot as he had. Bob looked at me and then he stared back up to my dad winking with a sparkle in his eye. "Now I'm not sure that I can get any of those pills because they are very expensive, but I'll see what I can do. If I can get any I'll give them to your father the next time I see him at the studio. So you make sure that you ask him, all right?" He smiled so wide that I'm sure his mouth hurt the next day.

I nodded my head. "I'll make sure I ask my dad."

I'm sure my father appreciated that, as I probably bugged him for months asking if he had brought the pills home. Even at that young age it took me a long time to forget about some things, especially something as important as pills which made you invisible.

****

As I grew older, my father indulged my childhood fantasies with the humor and energy of a much younger father. He realized the importance of invisible friends and the role-playing fantasies as a healthy part of maturation and learning processes for all children. You know, thinking back, my dad had a pretty good imagination, too. He seemed to play along with such ease to the fantasies that my sister and I crafted. At my age now I am aware that this might have been more than a little difficult than it appeared. It's not hard to figure out. My father didn't have kids until he was in his fifties. Granted my mother was twenty-one years his junior. I used to tease him about that. I used to tell him he had robbed the cradle. He usually smiled and nodded his head. They were a good match for at least as long as I have been alive.

My friends always loved spending time with my father. He was pretty funny. He was also full of stories which never failed to entertain the most tough-to-please of my friends. He watched as the world changed around him with an ease and an attitude I hope I am able to approximate as I get to sixty or seventy — or beyond if I'm extremely lucky. It is far too often and too easy to mouth the words without really being able to follow them. My father taught me that lesson by example.

Over time things change. A minor truism which many of the anti-evolution crowd seems not to embrace; but, in life it is a fact which must be addressed if you are to survive and succeed. He also taught me that your attitude is the one great equalizer when all around you changes. Acceptance of the nature of the world and a willingness to do your part to make it better.

We were in Palm Desert when this happened. I was frustrated about something, although I cannot recall what it was. My father handed me a slip of paper. "Learn the wisdom in this. It will serve you far better than anything I might say at this moment."

I looked at the paper and the words inscribed on it.

My father smiled ever so slightly and repeated the words to me. "God grant me the serenity to accept those things I cannot change . . . courage to change those things I can and wisdom to know the difference." He smiled more widely when he finished. That is the reforming alcoholic's creed. I saw it years ago and it seemed to be valuable so I keep a copy, where I can look at it frequently.

I looked at him puzzled at the reason he felt this appropriate for me at the moment.

He shook his head. "Read it over a few times and see if it doesn't give you a fresher outlook on your problem. I think you will find that if you take those words to heart, your life will be fuller and less frustrating."

In looking at my father as he had spoken that creed there was a wisdom in him which struck at me.

In dealing with the world at large and people specifically he was more than a little correct. That motto has been rolling around in my mind since then and my attitude has reflected it. When dealing with people it is important to have a good attitude, as in many instances there are only some things you may change. Other things just have to be accepted.

In that light I know my father had to have a good sense of humor. So many people wanted so much from him. Sometimes the demands that were placed upon him were more than I think one man could bear, and yet I never saw him get angry. He just smiled and let it roll off his back. I think if he were still alive and had heard some of the things said about his relationship with Howard Hughes and Cary Grant, he would do the same. He was never a man to make a big deal out of things that were inherently flawed and false. I admire that capability since my first instinct in the past might have been to stand up and try to argue or debate the falsity of a given statement. To do that gives the charge a backhanded validity which it doesn't deserve.

It mattered to him what people thought about him. That view of himself was tempered by the confidence he had inside. If he knew his feelings were justified and true then he simply passed off the comments of others as uninformed. This attitude came from his sense of what was right and of what was wrong. I know he must be chuckling now somewhere in the place he believed was heaven.

He never viewed himself as seriously as some others did and I guess still do. He was a man doing a job. As he has done almost everything in his life, it was a job for which he gave his best effort. He felt that was expected. He took pride in what he accomplished but it never went to his head. He was after all just a man who at times had the capacity and the ability to laugh at himself and the occasional events that he chose as his course. Maybe, too, it takes a well-founded sense of humor and irony to look at your fame and still be able to see that with or without it you are the same person you always were.

Chapter 5

FAMILY

Acting can be a very time-consuming occupation. In the days when Randolph Scott was at his peak in popularity which, from what I have observed and been told, extended from the early 1930s to the mid-1960s, it must have been tough on personal relationships and families as well. I know there were times when I was growing up that my father would leave for work before I rose in the morning. I am very sure of this because for the majority of my life I have gotten up by six a.m. almost every day and Dad had already left for the day. At the same time he would come home sometimes well after dark and occasionally long after my sister and I were asleep — long hours regardless of what the nature of the occupation.

The movie stars of that bygone era didn't command the huge paychecks that are given readily to many of the stars who currently grace the screen. My father was fortunate in that he was never without a film to make. He never was caught up in the glitz and hype. Certainly he partied with the best of them when he was young; but, the industry for him was a means to make money. The accessory hype was just that. He would never allow it to affect him. His privacy was far too important to him. I think that added to his mystique and somewhat to his popularity. People like me could identify with someone who lived as unassumingly as the characters he played in his films.

Of course in all the years when my father was among the top-ten actors, he was never without a contract or an obligation from one of the major studios. More than once he told me never to look to the motion picture or television business as a way to make a living. The long hours and the intensity with which he performed tired him as you might imagine. But, it never kept him from spending a great deal of quality time with his wife or his children.

I know there were times when he came home at night that the last thing he needed was to spend several hours playing with my sister and me. Yet, without respect to his waning energy level, he did. I was too young in those days and too inexperienced to have appreciated the effort he made to spend time with us. Forty years and a great deal of experience later I can see quite clearly how much he took upon himself to have a solid relationship with his family. He was principled in his outlook of his responsibilities and he was determined to share in the experience of his children's development and maturation.

In my heart I am sure that there were times he stalled or rearranged shooting schedules to correspond with special events he didn't want to miss in my sister's and in my life. I cannot recall him ever missing more than one or two pageants, school plays or any other semi-important happenings in my youth and adolescence. Considering his popularity at the box office and the number of films he produced it's amazing to me that he had any time at all. Few other occupations require the time away that acting does, because not necessarily all of the work is done at the studios. A great portion is done on location. Then there are the vast numbers of hours that must be spent on the script in memorization since actors were expected to know their lines, and editing if it was necessary for the continuity of the character. Under that kind of pressure it must have been difficult indeed to have found the time to participate in his children's lives.

****

There were very few father-son activities which I really wanted to partake in during my years in grade school, although there certainly were a few. Not one of them stands out in my mind at this moment so let's skip ahead to junior high school.

Seventh grade is an awkward, frustrating time for most adolescents and, trust me, I was no different. I hadn't thought of it before, but in those days my father seemed to sense my feelings of frustration and awkwardness. I was attending Harvard Military Academy in the San Fernando Valley. The school decided to host a father and son bowling tournament. I'm not really sure what possessed me, but I just had to be in that tournament. I knew that all of my friends from school and their fathers were going to be in attendance. I didn't want to be the odd one. Even with that consideration, I'm still not sure why I had to be in it because at that time I didn't know how to bowl. Since then I have been bowling off and on and I'm still not certain why I wanted to learn how to bowl.

My father was working on a film at the time and couldn't be home during the day, but he agreed to make allocation to go to the bowling tournament. He said he would try to arrange for me to learn to bowl in the few weeks before the time we would have to go. I know he meant well, but considering his shooting schedule, I wasn't sure. Things looked pretty desperate for a while as my father could not find the time during the day to take me to the bowling alley for me to learn how to play. Thank the stars my mother, who was always ready to pitch in with the game plan if Dad couldn't, decided that she would take me to the bowling alley in Santa Monica.

She went through a great deal to make sure I knew how to bowl before the school sanctioned father/son night at the bowling alley just a few blocks from the campus. She hired a young man whom she encountered at the bowling alley to teach me. I was too focused on learning how to bowl to have noticed much more than the ball rolling down the alley; but, I think, the teacher had designs on my mother. She sluffed it off as I'm sure she had done when she was younger when other men approached her. She was — and still is — a beautiful woman after all. The end result was that she made sure that she and I went to the alley several more times to practice before the tournament time arrived. I have to tell you that I was less than thrilled about going by then. I was frustrated and more than a little nervous about having to play considering my rather novice skills in the game.

I knew that I wouldn't bowl worth a darn that night even though I had practiced my backside off. I just knew I was going to embarrass my father and myself by my miserable performance. The night of the tournament I was as nervous as a cat on a hot tin roof. Dad was a little late getting home so, of course, I was worried that we wouldn't be at the alley in time, which might be a bigger embarrassment than playing badly. Couple that tension with the knowledge that I knew I wasn't going to be able to keep my ball out of the gutter and you have a traumatized child on your hands. It didn't matter, for when we got in the car it all seemed to be just fine. I could tell that my father had rushed home to attend this tournament. Most likely he had put off some things at the studio he had to do just so he could spend the evening with me. Through all the nervousness I felt very special that he was willing to go through so much just to keep his promise to me.

God, I was uncoordinated in those days. I had two left feet and three hands with no thumbs. We had a good time that night in spite of the fact that I bowled abominably. I think my dog could have bowled better, and he's never learned.

The last game we played was looking pretty good from my stand point until the last frame. I set up and let the ball fly down the alley. It hit the alley hard and then swept impotently into the gutter. I was crushed. I turned around and hung my head.

My dad was smiling but he understood. "Did you do your best, Chris?" I nodded my head weakly.

I know he must have chuckled inside. My face must have been hanging to the floor from the loss we had suffered. "Change your shoes, Chris. I think we deserve to go out for some ice cream." He stood up and put on the tweed sports coat which he had worn to the bowling alley.

I looked up at him for some sign that I had disappointed him but there was no trace. He just had a way of passing off this defeat. "Sure, let's go for ice cream." I thought for a second. "But we lost."

My father smiled sympathetically. "No we didn't. The fact that you gave it your best means that you won." What a great attitude! He wasn't just paying lip service either. He really meant what he was saying. I learned that about my father. He never said anything that wasn't true. When it came to this kind of thing, he believed firmly in the truth.

I guess I was a little uncoordinated in those years. Thank God I got past it. As I developed, I became much more capable and agile. It did seem as if the time it took was inordinately long. When you are young, many things seem to take on that dragged-out feeling. Fortunately for most of us it ends.

****

When you're young, I think, most parents tell you that no matter what and no matter where they will be there for you. My parents said the very same thing to me as I was growing up. I lived in a number of different cities once I got old enough to move out on my own but I never felt far away from my father. If I needed something, he made sure that I had it. Just the necessities, mind you. He didn't indulge my Gucci fantasies. (That's a joke.) It was a comfortable feeling to know that someone out there cared even though sometimes vast differences separated you. I went through a number of hard times before my father passed away. He may not have always been pleased with me, but he never let me feel as if I were alone and at the mercy of others. His attitude was just that. If I needed him, he would be there for me. To give you a small example, I was driving from San Diego to my apartment in what is now Century City. My car started acting funny after I passed through Carlsbad. By the time I reached Orange County my car had completely given out on me. I didn't know who to call or what was wrong with the car. I was eighteen at the time and had little experience with cars . . . that is the mechanical aspects of how engines function. I grew up in Beverly Hills where I didn't need the knowledge. Only when I was away from home for a few years did I finally learn more about cars.

I called my father even though it was past midnight. "Dad, I've got a major problem." I was in a strange area with no money, no credit cards and obviously little luck. Even the pay phone I used to call my father was more than three blocks away from where my car finally quit.

His voice was filled with concern. "What's the problem,

Chris?"

"Well, I'm not exactly sure, but the car just stopped running and there are not any service stations open." Past midnight in some areas can be treacherous. "Tell me where you are." His voice showed concern. He knew approximately the area were I was stranded.

I told him what off ramp I had taken.

My father's voice was calm and reassuring. "You stay in your car and I'll be there as soon as I can."

I hung up the pay phone and walked back to my stranded vehicle. In a little less than an hour my father pulled up in his old 1965 Thunderbird. He took me back to my apartment and said he would help me make arrangements in the morning to get my car towed to a service station. You know other people might have sent someone else but not my father. It was the middle of the night and Dad was not a young man at that time. He was in his seventies. I can't think of many men that age who would have been so quick to respond.

That incident gave me a great deal of comfort in later years. I knew that if I needed anything my father would always be available to lend at the very least a sympathetic ear if not a helping hand. It is hard to admit but I required his help far more often than I consider reasonable. There was a long span of time when I got myself into more binds than certainly I would have tolerated from a son. Still, my father was there for me through it all. I am very grateful for that.

****

To this day I watch my dad's movies. It's as if I still have a piece of him around for a short visit. People who know who my father was tell me how wonderful a man he was and how they grew up watching his movies. He made a distinct impression on at least a few generations of people on more than one continent. He never gave interviews and he tried never to allow the business that supported us over the years to affect us. He felt that his personal life was his to share and not the domain of everyone who had a question or anyone who wanted to know something. Even in writing this book I have to be careful not to infringe on the rights and the privacy of both my mother and my sister. This is an accounting of my relationship with my father, the thoughts we shared and the experiences I had with him. The only reason for sharing the very few tidbits of information about any of the rest of the family is to make a point that I wouldn't be able to get across without mentioning their partici- pation. In that way the privacy which my father guarded so jealously will not be compromised.

When I was nineteen years old I went to a showing of "Mame" starring Ann Miller. My mother knew her and was nice enough to arrange for my sister and me and our significant others to attend. After the show we were given back stage passes to visit with Ms. Miller. In the process of going back stage we ran into one of the famous talk show host sidekicks, who shall remain nameless as his privacy is important to me as well. He made a comment that my father should come on his show and give an interview. I stored that comment away and the next week when I saw my father I decided it was worth asking a more generalized form of that question.

With my sometimes overly enthusiastic manner I walked into my father's room. He was sitting in his chair reading. The light from the window behind him was his illumination. "Hey, Dad. How come you never give interviews?" I asked less to be flippant than to understand his reasons. There were a great number of people who I thought would be interested in his views and opinions.

My father turned in the chair where he was seated. "It's no one's business." He thought for a moment and then continued. "There are a few people to whom I would consider giving an interview but there is a catch. If I give one to them then I am obligated to give interviews to all the others. It's better if I don't give any interviews." He smiled. "Besides, I'm old news. I doubt that there are many people who would want to hear anything that I have to say." Considering his box office appeal and the number of films he had made, that seems to be a very modest statement.

I watched his eyes as he spoke. There was no feigning in the assertion or the attitude that he was nothing special. He was serious. He really thought that people wouldn't find much value in his comments. I know he also wanted to keep to himself those things which he considered private and didn't want them approached — even in a superficial way. Keeping his family away from the prying eyes of the public was his way of protecting us. He had never fallen prey to the need for overt publicity . . . not while he was alive in any event. It seems that after his death there are a few who have given him a little negative press but that is beside the point. I believe it's difficult to be in the spotlight because of your occupation. Little of your private life is safe. People are interested in their heroes and in the people who litter the screens with their images. Can you blame them? Knowledge of your screen idols makes them seem a bit more real. There is a real price to be paid for that knowledge by the person from whom it comes. It is invasive and can in some instances be dangerous, if not physically then at least mentally. It is even more difficult to have your life in the spotlight if your family is also subjected to the scrutiny of the press and the gossips as well. I am more than a little thankful that Dad managed to keep us away from the prying eyes and lenses which caught so many other families. In this way he protected our identities so that we could lead more normal lives in comparison to those others who were caught up in the limelight and basked in the attention which publicity can offer. It seemed to me that the children of those families lacked common perspective which I think my father gave to me by not indulging in the glitz. The last thing I would have wanted as I was growing up was for some of the things I did to make their way into the public eye. I would have been mortified.

If you think about it, that flash and glitter must have been at least a little seductive as so many others have given in to it. My father's ego and attitude were more solidly rooted and well founded to have been subject to the allure. He had fun to be sure in his time, but it was always well out of the view of those who wanted to splash it across the pages of the tabloid papers.

****

All actors of note are occasionally asked to participate in special events. At least in my father's day they were. It might be a pain, but it is a courtesy to the public who creates and pays the price for their livelihood. After all, without people to pay the toll for the tickets to the movies, they wouldn't be performing. It is the dues you pay for prominence and success in the field. My dad tried to steer away from those kinds of activities if it were possible, but there were times when it could not be avoided. Such was the case of the parade held in Palm Springs, California, which is near Palm Desert. I believe this particular parade was in 1956 or 1957. The parade organizers asked Dad to be the Grand Marshal. He agreed but asked if I, his son, could be allowed to ride with him in the parade as the Deputy Grand Marshal.

I was thrilled! I had been riding horses since I was old enough to sit straight in the saddle. I couldn't wait. I was also very proud that my father wanted me to be in the parade with him. By the time the parade was over, however, I think he probably questioned the intelligence of that decision. I did nothing bad, mind you, but as I stated earlier it was more than a little easy to distract me at that age.

My father's favorite horse was Stardust. This wonderful beast was in many of his films. He was a large dark Palomino with four white socks on his legs, a beautiful flowing white mane and tail and a white blaze on his face. I had expected that my father would ride that horse and that I would be relegated to another horse from the stable in Palm Desert where we rode most often when we visited there. To my surprise when we arrived at the parade staging area, they handed me the reigns to Stardust. He's the horse on which I learned to ride. I was ecstatic. I had to have a little help getting into the saddle as Stardust was a large horse and I was still very small. I looked around from my perch for a glimpse of my father. He was walking toward me with a horse that looked just like Stardust in tow. It seems the organizers wanted to find a close twin to his own horse.

My father and one of the helpers in the parade pinned my Deputy Grand Marshal's badge in my shirt. "Thanks, Dad", I yelled to him as he swung into the saddle of the horse he was to be riding. It looked so easy and natural the way he did that. Of course, he had the longest legs. That must have made it very easy for him.

He looked over at me. The sun danced over the contours and lines of his face and sparkled in his eyes. "Now, Son, I want you to stay close to me. You be sure that you wave at the

Marshal & Deputy Marshal before the Indio Parade

people along the parade route."

I nodded my head. I looked at him. This was great! I was going to be riding next to my father in a parade. He looked good, too. His dark tan cowboy hat had been pulled just the right distance down on his forehead. His leather tied shirt was accented with a western kerchief and the Grand Marshal's badge shining from the right side.

Dad smiled widely. Looking back in my memory it seems to me that there was great pride in his eyes. "That's my boy. You just don't get too far away during the parade." He knew me too well.

The parade started and I rode close to my father for the first quarter of the route. The color guard was just ahead of us and I rode with them part of the way until Dad took a little firmer control of my actions. After that I jockeyed back and forth between the color guard and him. I was dazzled by the people who crowded the streets along the route to watch the parade. I looked at my father frequently, partly because I didn't want to get into trouble and partly because he was an inspiring sight. He sat so tall in the leather saddle. The others who were on horseback in the parade also sat tall in the saddle, but there was something indefinably different about my father. As he had ridden when we went to the mountains, so did he ride in the parade. His back was straight and his shoulders were square as he rode the length of the parade route. As I see it in my mind he was the epitome of the old time cowboy and Western lawman. In a different time he might have looked the same and commanded the same respect.

He was confident but this wasn't exactly the difference between the other riders and my father. I guess he was majestic in a subtle, humble, special way. Looking back, it may have been that humility and genuine lack of pretense which made him seem so much different. His actions and manners seemed natural. He was to have been the star of the parade and yet to have talked to him you would never have known it. There was no arrogance or expectation in his manner or his voice. It was Randolph Scott paying tribute to the many people who have paid to see his films. It may have been his Southern upbringing and manners. (I have been living in the South for a few years now and the manner and the demeanor I saw in my father is evident in many of the people I deal with every day here — not so much in the younger Southerners but definitely in the older people I have met who call North Carolina their home.)

I remember that day very well. I can still see my father's ruddy complexion glowing brown in the sunlight of that day. I still see his big smile as he waved to the people along the parade route. I well remember the twinkle in his eyes as he looked into their faces. They responded to him in a way that I think is unique, which is in part the way he acted toward them. He didn't feel or act above them as so many in the movie industry do these days. He was appreciative of the public. They, after all, were the reason he was where he was. I cherish that most of all about him. What was most important of that event to me was less the notoriety of having been in the parade with my famous father than the fact that he wanted me to share it with him. I have to tell you that I was more than a little proud to have been his son . . . not just at that moment but all the ones before and after to this day.

****

Pick up any of the tabloid papers these days and you will read dirt about some famous person's marriage being on the rocks or maybe a certain celebrity was sneaking around on his wife or her husband. That kind of sensational story was in great abundance in my father's time as well. I think some of the only differences between then and now is that then the studios at times arranged for those stories to run. The philosophy was that the controversy might entice people to come and view that actor's or actress' current film. Now most of what you read is delivered and dug up by reporters looking to get the goods on someone. If the headlines on the market tabloids are any indication, facts are less necessary than the shock value of the accusation.

I find it unsettling that so much is said about events and attitudes of the past. We live in different times yet we seek to judge past actions by standards of a more modern and enlightened society. My, how the passing of a few decades can alter the way certain things are perceived. What used to be considered flamboyant and roguish is now contrary and appalling. The sad part of it is that some of the same people are making the judgments. I find that a little two faced.

My sister and I were too young to have paid much attention to that sort of drivel when we were young. There are times ,I have to admit, that I used to love to listen to my mother and father comment about some of the other personalities who either worked with my father or were in some way popular at the time. It was interesting. The point to be made here is they never expressed those opinions in public. As I got older I couldn't help but listen to the gossip which occasionally floated from the lips of my parents' friends. You know, friendly get-togethers sitting conversing in our living room, or at a party to which I might have been dragged to fulfill my family social obligations. There are times if I had had the courage and the temerity, I think I would have been tempted to buy a gallon of cream and drag out some saucers. They were at times just a little catty. Let's face it — Hollywood and the people who populate its films have been known to be a little, shall we say, indiscreet about their affairs.

As much as most of us are reticent to admit it, actors and actresses are people. They have faults and foibles. Heroic as they may seem on the screen some of them have feet of clay. It may be interesting to know their faults but I can see little reason to label them negatively. If they were regular people with more normal occupations you would react differently. I mean if a co-worker liked to drink heavily you might like him or her well enough, but you might not want to associate with that person outside of work. It doesn't make them bad. It just means they have different likes and needs. Regardless, you wouldn't go out of your way to tell everyone you encountered about that person's problem. That same problem might belong to someone famous and all of a sudden it becomes national news. That is patently ludicrous.

I never heard anything said about my father or my mother. I think that goes back to his not indulging in the glamour of his industry. Also there was nothing to say. Dad was the one who had to take trips to locations as a function of his movie career, and in later years for his business and his infrequent trips to the Mayo Clinic for health reasons. In all the time I watched my parents the only thing I ever saw or felt from them was love and trust for each other. I guess that set them apart from many other marriages in the world of celebrities. If either one of them led a secret life they sure kept it well hidden. Don't hold your breath; it wasn't their style.

They were not without their arguments and differences but somehow they were always able to work through their difficulties without the use of guns, sticks and other lethal devices. It was fun to watch them together, especially as I got older and was able to appreciate the love that was more than a little obvious between the two of them. Of course I found particular delight in watching the subtle battles which from time to time flared between them.

No, not battles as in yelling and screaming, but subtle wars for certain things. They were funny in that way. My mother loved chocolates . . . only milk chocolates. So did my father, but he would eat whatever he could find if he had the urge for something sweet. (As unfair it sounds, my dad was one of those people who could eat whatever he wanted and never gain extra weight. My sister was that way, as well. Only my mother and I had to be more or less careful of what we ate. My father could sit down and eat a box of chocolates and never gain a pound. My mother and I could just look at the box and gain a pound. It makes me wonder how she managed to stay slim throughout the years.) Every time my mom had a box of chocolates in her possession, my dad would get to it at some point and eat all the milk chocolates first. It didn't matter whether the box of candy was a gift or just a treat for which my mother felt the need, but he would find a way to devour all her favorites first. He would then eat whatever was left out in the open without complaint. He was, after all, a gentleman. What a devious little scamp he appeared to be at those moments! I got a charge out of it myself. It was the way he appeared when he did it with that twinkle in the eyes and that coy almost little boy smile. It was fascinating that such a distinguished and refined Southern gentleman could behave that way.

It has been many years since this kind of argument took place, but I can still hear my mother calling out to him from her room. "Randy, did you get into my chocolates?" She knew he had been the guilty person who stole her chocolates because neither my sister nor I were privy to her secret hiding places.

He would adopt this innocent little boy expression and stare into my mother's eyes. "Why no, Pat. I didn't even know you had any." I don't know how he said that with a straight face, because even as a child I knew that he always ferreted out my mother's treats. It was a game for him designed to lovingly annoy my mother. He really seemed to enjoy it.

Over time this argument escalated. Every time Mom would get a new box of chocolates, she would try to find a new place to hide it so that my father wouldn't know that it was in the house. Of course, she was always happy to share a piece or two with her children but she would be careful not to do so when he was anywhere close by. On occasion she would offer him a piece. He would smile graciously and thank her but you had to know that the next day when she went looking for a treat that some of the chocolates would be missing from the box.

Just when it appeared that she had found the perfect hiding place she would go to the secret location, open the box and then she would find that some of her favorites had magically disappeared.

I was in my late teens when I spotted my father walking out of his room chewing something. He smiled at me and he looked slightly guilty as if I had caught him doing something he shouldn't have been doing. I knew he had not been in the kitchen because I had just been there. I also knew that he didn't have any food in his room because that was not his habit. I was just about to say something to him when I heard my mother's voice. "Randy! Have you been into my chocolates again?"

My father winked at me and swallowed whatever treat had been in his mouth. He walked in to speak to my mother with a smug grin on his face. The scent of chocolate was distinct on his breath. Talk about outrageous. He actually walked in to talk to her and give her a kiss.

She used to get so mad at him for doing that. He'd apologize and swear that he couldn't help himself but it never stopped him from taking at least a few more of the candies he preferred. Personally I think she should have bought a decoy box and let Dad think he had found her secret stash of chocolate. If she did that very thing, I don't think it worked very well. From time to time I would hear her raise her voice in frustration as she stole to her hiding place and found the location to be less secure than she had thought. It was never real anger, mind you, but the kind of battle in which a number of couples I have known over the years indulged. I think some of this was my father's way of teasing Mom. He was a real tease and a genuine imp. At least he was to us.

****

Palm Desert in the 1950s and the 1960s had some of the finest golf courses and country clubs in the West. A great number of these clubs lay in close proximity to each other. It gave the golf vacationer a great deal of flexibility in where to play without having to endure a long drive. Of course, most of these clubs offered comfortable cottages or homes for either rent or purchase. As may be apparent from earlier sections, my father was truly passionate about golf. Guess where my family spent all of their vacations and holidays? Not much of a trick question is it? It was better than staying at home I suppose.

It worked out very well for us as many of the friends we had in Beverly Hills also took their vacations there as well. It was convenient, too, since it was only a hundred miles and change from our house. For Dad there was golf; for my sister and me there was a pool and tennis courts and the fact that there were a great number of children close to our ages; and for my mother there were all of her friends who didn't live in town as well as a large percentage of the ones who did live in the Beverly Hills area who were there. That meant that there was always someone in the adult category around to keep a watchful eye on the kids.

The first day we would arrive, and usually before we finished unpacking, my father would find some excuse or reason to either fit in a round of golf before dinner or, at the very least, go to the driving range. From then on, he would leave early in the morning to play. It's funny. From the earliest time that I observed him he seemed to like the early part of the day best. Maybe that was a hold over from having to be on the set early in the morning for so many years.

Dad had a way of making you feel important for some of the most seemingly ordinary things. Leng, the man who worked for my father in Beverly Hills, taught me how to cook the most rudimentary meals when I was about seven or eight years old — things like how to broil a steak and how to scramble eggs. He taught me in the mornings before the rest of the family was awake because I was always up at the same time he was and I expressed an interest in learning. When we traveled to the desert on holiday Leng rarely traveled with us. This was especially true after my sister and I were older than six or seven. For my dad that meant having to wait for my mother to rise before he got breakfast or he would have to eat at the country club dining room. More often than not Dad had an early tee time which meant that he would have to eat at the club.

I must have been about nine or ten when the following incident happened. It was around six or six-fifteen in the morning. I was busily reading one of my favorite comic books when my father walked out of the bedroom. He was dressed to play golf. I smiled at him. "Hi, Dad. Are you playing golf early?" I spoke in hushed tones because my mother usually slept a little later than that and I didn't want to wake her.

He smiled warmly at me as he passed quietly through his bedroom door. "Good morning, Christopher. Leng told me that he taught you how to make scrambled eggs. Would you like to make me some?" (I don't know if he was testing me but he had a look on his face which led me to believe that he was challenging me to show him what I could do.)

Now that was a silly question. Of course, I would make him some eggs. I didn't even look up at him . . . I just walked to the kitchen and went about the task of getting out the frying pan, the eggs, milk and butter. I liked cooking. Through the years I have become better than average in my ability to prepare a meal. As I think back to the cottage at the Eldorado I realize that the kitchen was not very well stocked with either spices or cookware. I guess my mother figured that we would be eating out more often than not with only a few exceptions. One of those was breakfast.

Dad watched me with interest as he made toast on the other side of the kitchen. "Are you sure you know how to do this?" I haven't really thought much about this incident over the years until I started writing this book. It makes my wonder if he was asking because I looked like I knew what I was doing or if I looked as if I didn't know up from sideways.

I turned to him in the middle of scrambling the eggs. "Yes, I do." I finished cooking the eggs and portioned them on to two plates so that both of us had some.

He inspected my handiwork before he lifted a small portion to his mouth with his fork. His eyes lit up as he tasted the eggs. He smiled widely. "Christopher, these are wonderful. How long have you been making eggs?"

"Leng taught me a few years ago." I spoke the words with pride as it was obvious that my father liked what he tasted and I had cooked.

His bright, impish smile crawled onto his lips. "You're going to make some woman very happy when you get older if you keep this up." He loved to tease.

"Aw, Dad. It was no big deal." I felt a little embarrassed by his comment.

Dad just laughed and after helping me clean up the kitchen left to play golf. It would have been unmannerly to have left a mess for my mother to clean up from his perspective.

From then on he would, from time to time, ask me to make eggs for him if he was up early enough. It made me feel very special and very proud. I wish I had a picture of the look he used to get when he asked, as well as when he had finished eating my eggs. You would have thought that I had just won the Nobel Prize because I doubt that he could have acted prouder. That's the way my father was. It was the little courtesies and the seemingly ordinary accomplishments which mattered to him. I guess he saw them as progressive stepping stones to other greater achievements.

****

Even though Palm Desert represented the time when my

father could more freely indulge his passion, he was also never very far away from his children. As he had done when we were at home, he always managed to spend a portion of his day talking with us or doing some things with us. I suppose it was only natural since he was a Western actor that one of the things he made sure we knew how to do was to ride horses. I liked riding with him even when I got older. It is the memory of when I was young and we went to Lone Pine which stands out so prominently in my mind. I enjoyed watching him ride almost as much as I liked watching Fred Astaire walk. They were both so damn comfortable and graceful in their surroundings.

Dad taught me to ride at the Hutchkin Stables in the San Fernando Valley long before it became the over-developed, smog-shrouded sprawl into which it has evolved. In those days that was also where he kept his horse Stardust. As I approached my teens, however, the only riding we did was in Palm Desert. The stable we frequented most often was Silver Spur. The man who owned it boarded private horses as well as the horses that could be rented by the hour or the day. On the days when my father would ride with my sister and me, he would often use some of the privately owned horses. He knew these people very well and, maybe because of his reputation as a horseman, they allowed it. Actually, I'm not sure how his riding of those horses came about, but suffice it to say that it did.

One horse he rode occasionally belonged to a Mr. Smith. I can't recall the gentleman's first name but he kept an unusually wonderful horse there during the winter months. Rex was a reddish masterpiece of equine breeding. His only problem was that he had three basic gaits: fast, really fast and hang on for your life. Dad liked riding Rex because the horse's spirit was slightly wild but controllable. I was well into my middle teens at the time and I preferred to ride with my friends. I think it disappointed my father when that transition began. Looking back I wish I had been more thoughtful and forward thinking to have spent more time riding with my dad. Out alone on the trail would have been a good time for us to stay close and maybe to avoid some of the more traditional pitfalls that occur between fathers and their teenage sons.

One day when I was fifteen, Dad took a number of my friends and me to the stables so that we could ride. As my friends and I saddled up, Mr. Smith walked up to my father and began talking to him. I had learned my manners well by that time and politely strolled up to the two men to pay my respects.

Mr. Smith turned to me and smiled. "Well, Chris. Are you as good a horseman as your father?"

I smiled shyly. "I'm pretty close." That was a lie but it was a challenge as well.

He handed me Rex's reins. "Why don't you give Rex a try?"

My father smiled and nodded to me to mount the horse.

Mr. Smith smiled up at me. "Chris, there are three people who can make Rex dance . . . your father, my daughter and myself. If you can make him dance, you can ride him anytime you want."

Rex was a big animal, maybe even half a hand larger than Stardust. As I swung up into the saddle and seated myself, I couldn't help but feel a little intimidated. I had been riding for better than half my life by that time and I was good. I wasn't sure that I could make the horse dance. I felt the horse beneath me. It was an unusual feeling to be on Rex. It's the difference I guess between sitting behind the wheel of a Volkswagen and a Porsche. I thought about it for a minute and then I pressed steadily but firmly on the rear ribs of the horse. To my surprise he danced. I shouldn't have really doubted myself; after all I had one of the best Western actors in the business as my teacher. I looked down from my perch on Rex's exquisite saddle.

Mr. Smith was smiling but my father was beaming. He had taught me well and he was proud. The two men spoke to each other in very hushed tones so I couldn't understand what they said.

Mr. Smith smiled up at me. "It seems as if old Rex likes you, Chris. If you would like to ride him it's perfectly all right with me."

I had joined a very elite club as Rex didn't like too many other people, and that was the reason only a few people had the opportunity to ride him. I rode that horse infrequently but it was always a pleasure. I owe my ability for handling horses to my father who spent the time insuring my horse skills would be appropriate for his son.

****

I've watched very carefully and at great length people who are out in public because people fascinate me. It goes back to my youth when I was shy. In those days I much preferred to watch as opposed to join. Countless times I have seen men and women cast a roving eye when their mates or partners are not looking. I spent a great deal of time with my parents in social situations, together and separately, and I have to tell you that I'm impressed. Neither of them ever did anything of which they could be ashamed or might be construed as untoward. To tell the truth I would never have expected them to have behaved in that manner.

From what I understand, once my father set his sights on my mother that was all she wrote. Some unions are destined to be. I think if that is true then my mother and father were among that select group. You didn't have to see it in person. A quick glance through one of my mother's great number of scrapbooks and you will see it quite clearly. The feelings and the love they held for each other almost jumps out of the photograph. I don't think you can fake it or pretend those feelings.

In his motion pictures my father rarely kissed his leading ladies. If you look at the progression of his films you will find that from the time he married my mother the few kisses he gave on screen diminished rapidly. I had a coach in high school who used to refer to my father as "no lips" because he never kissed his leading ladies. Some of the women with whom Dad made films were mighty good looking, too.

I once asked my father why he didn't have any more love scenes. I walked into his room where he was busily working at his desk. "Hey, Dad. I've got a question for you." I was being cute as I had seen him do so many times in the past. I figured I would get a rise out of him. I owed him a few from past teasing battles so I was hoping to get the score a little closer.

Dad took off his glasses and laid them on his desk. He

turned to look at me. "All right, Chris. Ask your question." He was smiling slightly because I'm sure he wasn't exactly sure what I had on my mind. I'm pretty sure he knew I was going to give him a hard time about something.

Clearing my throat I asked, "How come you hardly ever kiss your leading ladies? I mean it's embarrassing because you always ride off into the sunset with your horse and the woman is left behind. I realize the horses were well bred but you left some very fine-looking women alone."

He chuckled for a moment and shook his head good naturedly. "I'll tell you something, Son. After I married your mother I never wanted to kiss anyone else." A sly smile twisted his lips as he looked back to me. "Besides I don't think your mother would appreciate me kissing other women. What do you think?"

I looked at him for a moment. I didn't buy his answer completely but I think for the most part it was true. I nodded my head and then spoke after a moment of contemplation. "Maybe. But some of those women were awfully good looking. I'm not so sure I would be able to resist."

He laughed and gave me a playful slap to the gut. "Well, Son, that's the difference between you and me." I thought for sure that I had him with that one but as always he found some way to get around it.

My mother was a beautiful woman when she and my dad first met and married. To this day she is still a beautiful woman. The ravages of time and age seem to pass her by. I don't doubt that if she had been so inclined she could have easily found herself in films and been at least as popular as any of the screen vixens of that time. She, on the other hand, was quite satisfied with being a wife and a mother. She did well by her husband and both my sister and me. From a man's point of view, I can easily see why my father found her so desirable and he married her.

I guess that a good relationship begins with both partners having the ability to see the needs of the other and take them to heart. Having watched my parents through the years, I can attest that there were some compromises along the way but it never seemed as if they mattered. They did for each other without fanfare or expectation. My mother labored at her desk for many hours each day responding to Dad's fan-mail, taking care of my sister and me and attending all the functions which were important to my father. He, in turn, attended the functions which were important to my mother and spent time with her friends and their spouses. It was a real give-an-take life for the two of them. They were a prime example for my sister and me after which to model in our search for and expectations of relationships.

Have you ever seen two people in love glance at each other across a crowded room? You know they are at opposite ends of the room and yet the warmth of their feelings for each other just sweeps across to the other. I used to see that with my mother and my father. Dad would be talking sports or business with his friends and mother would be talking to her friends and making sure that everyone was accommodated and then they would look up at each other and ... God, what sparks they must have made together when they were younger.

Most of you are probably thinking that there were never any problems in this household but you would be more than a little wrong. Pat and Randy were as human as any other couple. They had their arguments and disagreements but they never seemed to last very long. My father counseled me more than a few times about successful relationships.

I can't remember what the girl's name was that I was dating at the time but I recall that she and I got into a huge fight. Dad overheard a little bit of it and sat me down to talk to me. "Is there a problem?" It was obvious by the expression in his face that he was concerned.

I was angry but his concern sidetracked my feelings for a moment. "How do you and Mom manage to get along?" I knew that they had disagreements from time to time but it never seemed to affect their relationship.

My father smiled slightly. "Chris, your mother and I make it a practice never to go to bed angry at each other."

It can't be that simple, can it? If it wasn't it sure seemed to work for them. Through the years I never caught any glimmer of anger from them the day after they had had a disagreement. I have a feeling he took his own advice. He and my mother never did seem to carry an argument beyond the time that it occurred. There is a lot to be learned from that ability to get along.

I said that my parents used to compromise and I think that was definitely true. I didn't get to see my parents at places like the country club dining room when there was dancing and we were in Beverly Hills. When we were in Palm Desert, I did see them. I don't think my father liked to dance very much, though I can't understand why. He was a good dancer. When my mother and he swept around the floor, they were a sight to behold. I think he felt uncomfortable in noisy environments because of his hearing. The din of the voices in the room coupled with loud music, regardless of its appeal or quality, made it very difficult to hear with or without the hearing aids that he hated wearing. In the days before my father's hearing went south, I'm sure that he used to take my mother dancing much more frequently and he probably enjoyed it far more. Still, they looked great together.

Uncomfortable or not, he did it and I think it was primarily for my mother's benefit. His relationship with her, for the more than forty years of their married life, was filled with little gestures of love and affection. It's been a while since my father passed away. Since that time my mother has shown no romantic interest in any of her male friends. I'm sure that she has had more than a few opportunities if she would have shown any interest. It seems that the men in her life are either related or just very good friends.

I was on the phone with my mother a few years ago. She was at her cottage in Palm Desert and I was at my home in North Carolina. "You know Mom, it's perfectly all right by me if you have a little romance in your life. I mean it's been quite a few years since Dad passed away."

I know that my mother was smiling as she spoke. "Thank you, sonny-boy but I don't think so. I just don't think that anyone else could fill your father's shoes. He is a very hard man to replace." Her voice was cheerful but it was obvious that she still missed my father very much. A love as strong and as long lasting as my parents' is something that stays with you.

"Yeah, I guess you're right, Mom." I guess that's true on a

number of levels. My father was and is a really hard act to follow. The love that he shared with my mother was easily one of those great loves that comes along only rarely. Too bad for the rest of us that it happens so infrequently. It is nice to know that it does happen.

****

As a parent Randolph Scott was the best although not perfect, as he did make his share of mistakes and misjudgments along the way. What do you know, he was human after all! There is no dirty laundry to be hung out in this section so don't get your hopes up. He did his best to make sure that my sister and I learned all that we could about his successes and his failures so that we would have a leg up on life before we had to confront it directly. It was his wish that we be both self-sufficient and competent when we left home to enter the less caring world of working and reality even though I know he wanted to protect us in every way possible.

He provided us the best education available for male and female children. He tried his best to educate us to our own individual needs for a good school education. One lesson he stressed was that anything can be taken from you.

I hated the times when report cards came out. It wasn't bad for my sister because she mostly got "A's". I, on the other hand, didn't do quite as well. One report card day my father came in to my room to have a chat with me. "Son, a few of your teachers had comments to make on your performance this semester. They think you are not working up to your potential. What seems to be the problem?"

"I don't know, Dad. I just can't seem to get the hang of some things." Actually I wasn't putting enough time into my studies so it was natural that some things wouldn't make sense.

My father shook his head. "Son, the one thing that cannot be taken from you is your mind. Everything you have or will have can be taken from you but not your mind. You would do well to make that the very best you can. I can't do it for you and it is the one thing I want most for you to have."

"Yeah, Dad, I know."

"I'm not so sure that you do. Your education and your ability to use your mind will make the difference between what you want to be and what you will be. You better take this seriously because the chances to learn go away if you don't take advantage of them."

I had to be in my thirties before I really appreciated the wisdom of that philosophy but I finally did. I think he'd be happy about that. It is amazing the difference education makes in your ability to see the world around you. Even people treat you differently when your mind is more exercised.

He was never unreasonable about his expectations of me. He saw, as few others ever have, that I was different and was able to adapt his view of me as a result. I think he was able to adjust his thinking to accommodate that. At least it seemed that way from the manner and sensitivity with which he dealt with me and the problems I encountered while he was alive. We had our ups and downs in the way we handled each other but over all we had a healthy respect for each other. I guess the best I can say is that my father was a fair man. At times he was quick to dismiss some things which I felt were of earth-shattering importance, but most of the time he would listen. He believed in that. He didn't have to agree with all that I said or believed because to him that was my right, and he expected that there would be times when I wouldn't agree with him, but he did expect to be extended the same courtesy by me to hear him out in his view and his opinion.

He respected well-thought-out ideas and actions. Even though he might not necessarily come to the same conclusion, he would give sufficient room in his mind to allow for the individual ideas of expression and follow through. Considering his age and the era in which he was reared, I think that he was pretty forward thinking and progressive in his outlook. Not in everything, mind you, but in a great majority of instances..

****

There is more than likely a great deal more to say about the way our family functioned as a unit but I don't really feel that is necessary. Randolph Scott was a very private man especially where it came to his family. I've probably shared more than is prudent but you would never have a proper perspective of the man if I didn't. There is more to be said about a number of different aspects of his life of which I have been fortunate to have been a part, so you as the reader will have to contend yourself with that. Out of respect for my father's insistence, there are some things which I would love to share but respect demands that I shouldn't.

Just know that there were no "Mommy Dearest"-type secrets floating around my father's skeleton closet. I'm sure there are those who would love to allude to that, however, as there is a great deal which I am not sharing, but believe me they are wrong. My father just didn't do bad things. He made mistakes but there were no insane or out of the ordinary histrionics in our family.

No, he didn't scream at us exclaiming at the top of his lungs, "I've told you! No more of those wooden hobby horses with synthetic manes!" And no, he didn't chase us around the house with a riding crop in order that he might beat us into submission.

The thing to keep in mind about Randolph Scott is that just like the characters he played on the screen, he was a fair and compassionate man. He treated his family as the treasure they were . . . his treasure. A day never went by that he didn't act according to that sentiment.

Chapter 6

FRIENDS

My father had some great relationships with a tremendous variety of people. To be sure his friends were an eclectic assortment of people from a diverse collection of occupations and backgrounds. There were some similarities, too. Each of the men with whom my father spent his time seemed to be cut from at least similar molds. All were successful in their own fields and each was a gentleman in his own right. They were not chauvinistic in their views but forward-thinking men who were, as far as I can see, at times ahead of the current level of thought. Yes, like my father, most of them were conservatives and with good reason.

This section is dedicated to introducing you to a few of them and the stories which their names evoke. I wish I could tell you about all of them but I think most of you will have little patience for a list that long. There were many more but the few I will introduce in this chapter are a good selection of the people with whom my father associated. Out of respect the introductions will be brief as their privacy is as important to them as it was to my father. I wish I had been born a few decades earlier so that I could have known more of his original friends in Hollywood. I'm sure it would have been a mind-opening experience.

Having discovered Randolph Scott when he first arrived in Hollywood, Howard Hughes, the president of RKO Radio Pictures, watched the young actor's career very closely and used him for a good

number of his studio's films. In his first few years he worked for Paramount in *Hot Saturday, Hello Everybody, Murders in the Zoo* and a series of Zane Gray Westerns, *Cocktail Hour* for Columbia, and *Broken Dreams* for Monogram. Of course, RKO featured the handsome newcomer in several films, including *Village Tale, She, Roberta* and *Follow the Fleet.* Several years later he co-starred in *My Favorite Wife, Bombardier* and *Belle of the Yukon* before starring in *China Sky.*

During the filming of *Roberta* and *Follow the Fleet* Randolph Scott and Fred Astaire struck up a close friendship which stretched through the rest of their lives. *My Favorite Wife* co-star Cary Grant likewise developed a life-long friendship with Randolph Scott after their first meeting in *Hot Saturday Night.* There was a magic between these men which was obvious on and off the silver screen.

****

First and foremost on my father's list of friends when I was growing up was Fred Astaire. He was a frequent visitor to our house and I got a real charge out of him. My father and he were a handsome and elegant riot together. I would like to have been privy to more of them as I got older but that was not to have been the case. It is enough that I was able to see them together in the first dozen or so years after my birth. There was a subtle magic that lay beneath the surface when the two of them were together. The contrast in their sizes added to that magic as well as comic effect to their friendship and the obvious enjoyment they had for each other's company.

Both men were devoted Dodger fans which meant that at every convenient opportunity they would scurry to the game together. When you see the two of them on film (with the possible exception of *Follow the Fleet*) they seem like such elegant and reserved men. From my own experience nothing could be further from the truth; that is, at least at the baseball games. They cheered and commented like everyone else. It isn't like they behaved out of character, it was just that they didn't show that side of their personalities very often. When they did, it was great and I can't tell you how much pleasure I got out of it. To see two such ordinarily dignified men acting like the rest of us kind of made the world seem a little less cold.

In most situations of a social nature they were gentlemen with their manners fully locked into the full time position, but there was something about them which belied that. To me it seemed as if there was an impish twinkle in the eyes that might erupt at any given moment . . . given the right circumstances and people around them. Most of it was subtle. It was buried in a wink or a knowing smile, but it was there. It didn't come out very much around me but there were a few occasions. It was a magical experience. The nice part is that around kids they had the capacity and the potential to join in without looking out of place.

I never saw the two of them play golf together but my mother says they used to play together as often as their schedules allowed in Los Angeles and the desert. I don't recall my father ever saying that they did but it has been quite a few years since then. I know that in the 1950s and the 1960s they had reasonably burdensome shooting schedules. It always seemed that the two of them were busy constantly. I think each of their personalities was well suited to the other's. One thing that I noticed about the two of them was the warmth that was exuded when the two of them smiled. They really smiled without restraint and it was infectious. If you were the object of one of their smiles, you just had to smile back. It was an involuntary reaction.

As was my father, Fred Astaire was a thoughtful man. He never forgot either my sister or me on birthdays and holidays. I can't remember that he ever showered us with gifts, but the tokens he remembered us with were special and unique. They were little reminders of him which to this day I value and cherish. Oddly enough he always did his own shopping when so many others in his position had others do it for them. It makes the gifts he gave us that much more special.

I don't know if this was always true, but like my father Fred Astaire was one of the most genuinely humble men I have ever encountered. For all his fame and elegance he was a man unfamiliar to conceit. He was such a marvelous performer and showman. How could he not have realized his contribution to the films he generated? Shortly after completing *Finian's Rainbow*, Fred was attending the world premiere. The interviewer stopped him as he entered the theater. Fred gave all the credit for the film's marvelous feel to Tommy Steele, Petula Clarke and everyone else but himself. Now I have seen many performers do that same thing but in those instances it felt and looked contrived. When Fred Astaire did it, it was genuine and from the heart. Those were his true feelings. No wonder he and my father got on so well.

I remember speaking to him just after that picture was completed. I was in my mother's room when he phoned. Out of courtesy my mother handed me the phone after she finished speaking to Fred. "Would you like to speak to your Uncle Fred?"

I took the phone from her and spoke. "Hey, Uncle Fred. How's the new picture?"

You could almost hear his smile from the other end of the line. "It's wonderful, Chris."

"Do you do any dancing in this film?" I asked because I have always marveled at the way he moved. As a matter of fact there were a number of us in those days who felt it might be worth any price to be able to walk like Fred Astaire and talk to women like Cary Grant.

He chuckled. "No, not any more, I'm afraid."

"Why not?" I couldn't imagine why.

He laughed for a moment. "It seems that either the women are getting bigger or I'm just slowing down, but I just can't seem to lift them around the dance floor like I used to."

It was a cute response, but then I rarely expected anything less from him.

****

Freeman Gosden and his wife Jane were two of the closest friends my parents had. To this day even though both Mr. Gosden and my father have passed away, Jane Gosden and my mother are still the best of friends. Freeman Gosden, for those of you not old enough to remember, was the creator of "Amos and Andy," along with another gentleman named Charlie Correll. On the radio show not only did Mr. Gosden write the scripts but he was the voice of the Kingfish. As I am a member of the Elks, I found it interesting to find out in conversation with Jane that Mr. Gosden had loosely modeled the lodge to which "Amos and Andy" belonged after the Benevolent and Protective Order of Elks. It saddens me to see the controversy which has been brought to light over that program. I knew Freeman Gosden all of my life and I doubt very sincerely that he intended it to be racial in his depiction of his characters. As a matter of fact there are some lessons in those old shows which still have merit today.

Like my father and many others who associated with him, Freeman Gosden was a man of conviction and fire. His beliefs and principles were not up for negotiation. Freeman Gosden was one of the few men I have ever met whose convictions were never in question. His principles and his sense of family were higher than most. In these days when we speak of family values, my father and Mr. Gosden were well ahead of the game. They held up their actions and words as testimony to that fact.

In Palm Desert when our two families were there at the same time, Mr. Gosden and my father would spend a great deal of time together on the course. (That's where we always went for holidays and vacations during fall, winter and spring. Summer in the desert isn't a fit environment. It's probably why you can't pay me enough to go there now. Well, that and the fact that I live three thousand miles away, are reason enough. It was a lot of fun when I was growing up anyway.) Mr. Gosden and my dad were very similar in a great number of ways and very different in many ways, too. Dad always seemed a little more serious when he was around Freeman. Then again Freeman Gosden was a more subdued and restrained personality than my father. Still, I have it on good authority that Mr. Gosden spent a good deal of time with Dad in the early days when my father lived at the beach in Santa Monica. I never would have guessed that the two would be friends. That may be because I never got to see them in their younger days. I think that speaks for my father's ability to see past the cover and to take from inside the real values and attributes.

One thing they did have in common were their sons, who both men loved and cherished. I think between Craig, Mr. Gosden's son, and me we caused both men to tear their hair out from time to time. To be sure, when we were teenagers we drove them the craziest, especially when we were on the golf course or when we drove our cars around the perimeter of the Eldorado Country Club.

It was Thanksgiving vacation in 1966 when Craig and I decided to have a race around the back road of the club after we had been at the club for a few days. My father and Mr. Gosden had received several complaints from some of their friends who had witnessed our little impromptu race.

My father walked into my room with a scowl on his face. "Chris, I've warned you about how fast you drive that car around the club grounds. I want to know whose idea it was."

I hung me head. "I'm sorry, Dad. It was my idea." I hadn't really considered the consequences of what my father would say if he found out about our race.

He crossed his arms. There was no great anger in his eyes but it was painfully clear that he was upset. "I want you to call Mr. Gosden and tell him." He didn't yell. Yelling was not the way to get his point across. He felt that if he told me his feelings about my behavior I would see his logic and do the right thing.

I did and Mr. Gosden chastised me for a few minutes but ultimately he forgave me. They were always getting after Craig and me for doing one thing or another.

Freeman Gosden and my father talked a lot about business and expectations. Both were very shrewd and took advantage of favorable business opportunities. Both men tried to give us the benefit of their wisdom through the years and I think that they gave us some powerful insights which neither of us would have received without them.

My father and Freeman Gosden were the kind of men to whom you could go and talk if you needed advice. They would listen to a problem without necessarily allowing their personal feelings to interfere. I appreciated this aspect of Mr. Gosden's and my father's friendship. On a number of occasions I had to draw upon that ability from both of them. Like my father, Freeman Gosden was a busy man but he always seemed to have time to talk if you expressed an interest in his opinion. Sometimes he was a little harsh but he never refused to give you the benefit of his wisdom if you asked for it.

In social situations greater than just family get-togethers I watched them as they made their way through the people in attendance. Each man was as socially graceful as a ballet dancer and as tough as a defensive linebacker when there was a point to be made. They knew the answers to so much that it amazed me. Neither of these men had tolerance for boisterous and arrogant people. I think it unsettled their natures, especially the people who were more than willing to give advice when it was apparent that that person had no idea of the facts and realities of the situation.

****

There are some people who in their journey from birth to the grave add to their roster of friends great minds, statesmen, politicians and presidents. My father was one of those. For the life of me I cannot understand why he was not pretentious or boastful about his friends. He must have known that only a few people in the world are allowed to call some of these people friends. He never acted as if it were important. They were just his friends and it mattered not that they were among the powerful and the famous. Listed high among the names of his good friends was Dwight David Eisenhower. I looked up to this man for his vast intellect and sensitive manner. He was another of those unpretentious people with whom my father enjoyed spending his time, especially at the times when the two were free and in the same locale. I found his humility of his place in history and the unaffected manner of his spirit even though he played a significant role in the history of the twentieth century — incredible. Of course, It is not often that you get to socialize with a man who is listed prominently in the history books you are studying in school. Maybe it is that aspect of the man which makes me think he should have had a more self-

Freeman Gosden and Dwight Eisenhower

centered perspective of himself, but he didn't. I think he long before had come to terms with his role in the history of our country and the world and had decided to accept it with humility and grace as he had done most of his life.

Serendipity doesn't happen too terribly often in a person's life. I know that in my own I've normally been left with a sense of wonder as to how it happens. Usually I'm just glad to have recognized it at the time. That is the way in which my parents first met the General and Mamie Eisenhower. It seems that in their travels across the United States my parents crossed paths with the Eisenhowers. My father had gone to the Moncrief's Gunnison Ranch In Colorado. My mother was unable to attend as she was in bed with a cold, so she was stuck in the Brown Hotel. Unfortunately her room was part of a suite which was taken over by President Eisenhower. This meant that my mother had to move out of her room. Fortunately she had friends in the hotel. Former Texas Governor Dan Thorton's wife brought her over to her suite. It wasn't until she was at the Thunderbird Country Club in Palm Desert that my mother was introduced to the man who had caused her to vacate her room in the Brown Hotel. She was introduced to the General by Leonard Firestone. The next time she and my father made the General and Mamie's acquaintance was at the Seely Mudd cottage at the Eldorado Country Club. From that moment forward they became good friends even though they lived on opposite ends of the country. Of course, the General and Mamie had a house in Palm Desert at the Eldorado Country Club, as did my mother and father.

My parents spent time with the Eisenhowers whenever they were in the desert up until the time that the General passed away. After that we saw very little of Mamie but my mother kept in close touch with her until she, too, passed away. I always liked the General and Mamie. They treated my sister and me, as well as all the children of their friends, as if we were family. Actually at the desert, Craig Gosden, David Eisenhower, the General's grandson, and I used to spend a lot of time together. Most of the time, however, the kids would go in one direction and the parents and grandparents would go in another. It's too bad. I didn't realize the importance of my time with the General while he was still alive. I was just too young to have seen it. Still I have some wonderful memories of my time with the Eisenhowers.

There was a time I can recall with vivid clarity. The Gosden's had invited my family to their house for a holiday get-together. When we arrived the Eisenhowers were already seated in the living room. I must have been about fourteen or fifteen years old which would have placed the year at 1964 or 1965. The adults congregated in the living room expecting to have the peace and quiet to carry on adult conversations.

Craig, our sisters and I were in the kitchen when Mr. Gosden and my father came in to talk to us. Mr. Gosden directed his comments to Craig and me. "The adults are going to be in the living room talking. If you want to come in and join us you may but I don't want you to interrupt." He was definitely directing his comments to Craig and me. The two girls were too young to be interested in joining the adults. Besides they had other priorities. It was the boys Freeman Gosden was concerned about. He knew us too well. We were at that age when you tend to open your mouth before you have fully thought out the ramifications.

My father just smiled without saying anything. I never was one to follow orders but I was willing to give it a shot. I went into the living room with Craig with every intention of abiding by my parents' and the Godsens' directions. When the conversation turned to Communism, as it did frequently in those days when a group of conservatives got together, I had to put in my two cents. I had to do it because I had written a paper for my history class just a few weeks prior. I had only intended to make one small comment but I must have monopolized the conversation with Dwight Eisenhower for the better part of thirty minutes. Mind you I wasn't trying to be rude or abrasive but I had some questions and comments that I felt were worth making. The General spoke to me as if I were an adult. He listened to me and talked to me without treating me as the teenager I was. I was thrilled to have been able to have had the opportunity to speak at length with him on a subject which was current and timely.

I found out the next day that Freeman Gosden was more than a little upset and put off with my behavior. I didn't find out that night because as we kids had had enough of the adults after my speech-making and we were off in search of more fun things with which to occupy our time. My parents took us home when their socializing had broken up for the evening.

The next day my father came to my room to tell me about his feelings about the night before. "Chris, I wasn't aware that you were so informed on the subject of Communism. You made quite an impression on General Eisenhower." I remember he chuckled slightly. "You're going to have to call Mr. Gosden and apologize to him. Unfortunately you made quite an impression on him as well. He was a little angry that you took so much of General Eisenhower's time." I was worried about having to call Mr. Gosden to apologize and my father seemed to think the situation was humorous.

I apologized. "I'm sorry, Dad. I didn't mean to cause any trouble but he was talking about something that I knew." I sighed heavily and glanced over at the phone.

My father smiled and patted me on the shoulder. "Well, you

did a very good job but call Mr. Gosden and apologize to him for interrupting the conversation anyway." He started to leave my room but turned back to me from the door. "By the way, Son, I was very proud of the way you handled yourself last night." Unlike Mr. Gosden he was anything but upset. He was proud of the way I handled myself in the conversation . He hadn't realized I was so well versed. I'm glad he was my father. Freeman Gosden was a fair man, but I think he was a bit more strict and less easy going about punishments.

****

Randolph Scott was a devoutly religious individual. Only illness or location work prevented him from attending worship services at All Saints Church in Beverly Hills. He wasn't a "bible thumper," but the principles of the Episcopal convictions were very close to his heart. Unlike so many others who cherished their beliefs on Sundays only, my father tried his best to live up to the Christian edicts and standards every day. He didn't cram his belief down your throat in conversation, but it was very evident in the way he conducted his life that his beliefs and adherence to the standards of the church were firmly in-grained.

Considering my father's status and taking into account his years in Charlotte, North Carolina, it seems a natural extension that he and the Reverend Billy Graham should have met and become friends, since Charlotte, North Carolina, was Billy Graham's hometown, too. I never realized just how religious my father was as I grew up until the first time I met Billy Graham. I sat in the living room of our house and quietly listened as the two men spoke at length about God and their beliefs. I was impressed. I wouldn't have sat quietly if that had not been the case.

Reverend Graham was a unique man to be around. He had, and I'm sure still has, almost a tangible glow about him that I have seen only a few other times in my life. You can't help being at ease in his presence. His eyes are so warm and kind. He is like no other man I have ever encountered. I know that my father felt that way about him. If I were a more religious man, I would have relished the opportunity to have prayed with Reverend Graham as I know my father did.

Billy Graham is a man of remarkable patience and humor. Very little seems to ruffle his feathers in his contact with people. There was one incident which springs to mind. It's times like this that I wish I had a videotape so that I could be more complete and specific. So many of the details have been washed away and bleached by the passage of time. (I will apologize to my sister before I continue with this story. Ordinarily I might not share this, but it is just too good to pass by and not relate some of it.) My family and Billy Graham were sitting at the dining table in the lanai of our house eating lunch. I was in my early teens and my sister was just approaching her teenage years. About halfway way through the meal my sister announced that she didn't believe in God. I expected Reverend Graham to lose it, but he just smiled and questioned my sister about her statement. I thought my father was going to fly out of his chair at the statement but he, too, just sat and listened to the comments. As I stated, I really wish I had been in possession of a video camera that night but they hadn't been invented yet.

I know Dad was a little embarrassed by my sister's pronouncement, but he took it in stride as did Billy Graham. They laughed about it later as I watched them conversing on the couch. Their beliefs were not affected by those kinds of comments. I can see why so many people follow Reverend Graham in his crusades across the face of the Earth. When he speaks about his beliefs and delivers his sermons, there is something indefinable which occurs in you as you listen to him and watch his face. I just can't put my finger on it. It floats around him like an aura. It attaches itself to his words and they just sort of flow inside you. Listening to Billy Graham and watching him is one of the most amazing experiences I have ever had.

I am truly appreciative of my father's relationship with Billy Graham. Occasionally, in the last years of his life as his health was beginning to fail, Reverend Graham would fly out to visit my father and pray with him. At that time Dad was not well enough to attend church as he had been accustomed to in the earlier years of his life, so I think the quiet prayers he said alongside his friend meant more to him than all the church services he had ever and could ever have attended. This speaks of the affection and friendship which flourished inside Billy Graham for my father. I think, if it is possible for two souls to touch, my father's and Billy's did during those prayers in my father's room of our home.

So important was my dad to Billy Graham that he felt it necessary to say the eulogy over him at his funeral. I wish I could have had a record of it or at least a copy of the words. Unfortunately the words Reverend Graham spoke were not rehearsed or written down as much as I might wish they had. They came from his heart while he spoke those words over my father's casket. The words and the sentiments that went with them were a fitting testament to a man who touched millions of people in his lengthy career as an actor and a businessman.

Like Dwight Eisenhower, Billy Graham's time with my father was only occasional as both men were extremely busy in their different ventures. Reverend Graham's visits were all too brief when I was young, but when I was older I was not close enough to just run over and spend time with him. In both of those men I had the opportunity to stand before true greatness. My dad attracted those kinds of friends and I can tell you for a fact that my life has been enriched by my acquaintance with both of them. In retrospect I doubt that my father ever thought about the status of the friends he amassed throughout his life. I think he saw himself as ordinary and that his friends were just that . . . his friends. It didn't occur to him that he and the men and women with whom he associated were any different than anyone else. But they were, and it speaks to the character and intelligence which my father possessed, which made him attract that caliber of person to him.

****

There were a great number of people to whom my father was close in the years before my sister and I were born. I guess that happens with friends who span a great number of decades. You remain close,. but distance and obligations keep you from the bond you once might have shared. We never had much contact with Cary Grant, but my father had an endless number of humorous stories he used to tell us about the days with Cary when they were new to the movie industry. They used to share a house on the beach in Santa Monica. From the information I gleaned from the stories all those years ago, Cary and my father were quite the rogues with the ladies at the beach. There were quite a few times when some of the women who knew both men at that time, and are still friends of the family, have said that those two really knew how to throw a great party.

The house where Cary and my dad resided in the 1930s and the early 1940s had long since been sold by the time I was old enough to go to the beach. I have walked by the house a number of times as a teenager when I was learning to surf and watch girls on the beach. I understand why they lived there. It had a pool with a wall separating it from the beach. If the crowds of people I saw in the 1960s were present even by half that number; then, there would be a large number of eligible young ladies walking by to back up some of the stories I heard. I tend to think that many of those stories are greatly exaggerated; but, even if that is the case, at least some of them have to be at least a little valid. I can't imagine two men as good looking and available as Cary Grant and my dad not generating some roguish stories about their female guests.

From many of the stories I have heard, Cary, Freeman Gosden, my father and a number of other actors who were prominent in those days all spent an inordinate amount of time at the beach house. I never heard any negative or derogatory comments, so I assume that they must have had a good deal of fun — but nothing that would be considered out of the ordinary.

I had originally promised myself that I wouldn't jump on a soap box in this section, but I can't help it. Please forgive me if I sound too much like I am preaching.

A few years ago a book came out which tried to imply that my father, Cary Grant and Howard Hughes might have been gay. It amazes me in a sort of twisted way the lengths to which some people will go to try to make money from people who are no longer alive. In the book they cited the beach house as the location where at least some of that alleged activity took place. Nothing could be further from the truth.

My mother is one of those people who saves pictures in a library of photo albums. Not just pictures from her time with my father, but also the pictures which the studios mandated in the days before she even knew my father. We used to look at the older albums from time to time. It was fun to see how things had changed from those early years. Most of the photos which appeared in that cheesy book were publicity photos which had been taken and posed for by Cary Grant and my father at the request of the studio to which they were contracted at the time. For those of you who are too young to remember the Golden Age of film, publicity photos were a mainstay for contracted actors. I looked at those pictures a number of times in my youth as well as a great many other publicity-type photos of my father and Cary with some of the most beautiful women I have ever seen.

There are some factors to take into account as you view memories of this nature. Actually, anytime you look at evidence from the past there are a number of pitfalls to which you may fall prey. First, these pictures were posed for at the studio's request. These were not the kind of pictures that you or I might have taken as memories of our time together. They were posed and contrived. They hardly reflected the demeanor and attitude of the subjects. Someone was directing the poses from behind the lens of the camera. Somewhere along the line the pictures were designed to have a specific impact on the people who would be viewing them. Another valuable consideration of which you should take note is that pictures taken almost sixty years ago reflect a much different view of the likes and dislikes of society. Different times imply that there were different attitudes, governed by different views and perspectives of society which, by the way, were the movie-going public. You need not believe me. Just look around at how movies and styles have changed in the past few decades. For those of you old enough to remember miniskirts, you will also recall the trauma it caused in this society. It was going to bring about the moral decay of our youth. They are coming back in the 1990s and you don't hear that said any more. Times change. This has always been true. We have archaeologists to study the way people lived in different eras because they have the ability to determine the context of the evidence. You and I may not have that kind of insight.

Cary Grant and Randolph Scott in the 1930s and 1940s were sex symbols much like Kevin Costner, Sean Connery and Harrison Ford are to some people now. They were supposed to look "dreamy." As a consequence, that was the effect the photographer who took the pictures was trying to achieve. The pictures were taken with the perspective of that era in mind. I doubt that they would be taken in that manner if they were taken now.

You know, it occurs to me that in those days John Swope, Henry Fonda and Jimmy Stewart used to room together. No one has made any comments about them being gay. Of course none of them had the same reputation which Cary and my father had for garnering so many attractive young ladies either, although I'm sure that all of them had more than their fair share of attractive women.

The final factor you should think about is the fact that the pictures were taken from my family by a homosexual man who was fired as my father's nurse, who was supposed to be taking care of him as his health declined. The man was fired for dubious and poor performance of his job and inappropriate behavior. Those photos were accessible to anyone in the house, as the photo albums were plainly marked. The man took them, obviously out of spite because he was fired. I'm sure he gave no explanation of their nature, as he possibly didn't know for what those pictures were made. If he had known and had told the people to whom he sold them, they probably wouldn't have bought them. He most likely had no idea that these pictures were taken as publicity for a film which my father and Cary were making. It is a very old film now, but it was called *My Favorite Wife*. It was not a great film, but it was cute. It was designed to showcase two very attractive and handsome men, which it did very well.

I have been asked whether I thought my father was gay by a number of people, some of whom I would have thought knew better. I can tell you honestly, having grown up with him, that he was not gay. In my opinion, it seems that some people just like to muddy the water about people who can no longer debate the issue. It was never put forth when either of the men was alive. I can only judge the accusations to be false and slanderous. After all, how courageous is it to slander a good man when he is dead just so you can turn a quick profit? It takes a very small and intellectually cowardly person to attempt such a thing. The writers of that book, and any book like it, will never measure up to the standard and the success of the people they are trying to diminish. They are to be pitied and ignored, as their opinions are likely not to have much merit.

This is one of the problems of being in the public eye. No one would have thought anything of the sixty-year-old photographs if they had been of just average everyday people. They were not average or everyday. They were actors who were stars. Like that should make a difference. No matter how good or straight you are, there will always be someone who will misread the intention. I think that was the reason for my father's obsession about privacy. It is certainly the reason I am guarding the privacy of all the people I have mentioned in this book.

As far as I have ever known, Cary Grant has always been the consummate ladies' man — charming and graceful in social situations with an impishness that marks all true lovers of life and beautiful women. I saw Cary when I was sixteen years old and had taken a special young woman to Trader Vic's for dinner. I was going to do my best to impress her and Trader Vic's was the place to go for that.

I ran into Cary Grant on my way to the restroom and stopped for a moment to politely introduce myself. "Mr. Grant, I don't know if you remember me, but I am Chris Scott, Randolph Scott's son."

He looked at me for a moment and smiled. "Nice to see you, Chris. How is your father?" He had one of those smiles that you had to return in kind.

"He's very well, Sir." I didn't want to be rude and keep him from his dinner companions, so I cut short any comments I might have felt like making. "It was nice seeing you." I went my way and he walked off in the direction of his table. There is no doubt that he was a charming and good-looking man.

About forty-five minutes later I was failing abysmally with my date. I couldn't seem to crack the ice which had developed around her. I had tried the very best I knew how to impress her but it seemed to be all for naught. At the rate I was going, the kiss I was hoping for at the end of the night might not even be a handshake.

Cary walked by and looked down at us. I think he saw the desperate nature of my plight. He stopped. In his charming way he spoke to me and introduced himself to the young lady. "Why hello, Chris. This must be the charming young lady you were telling me about." He winked at me and turned to her. "My name is Cary Grant." He held out his hand to her and I thought she would faint right there. I can see why women used to swoon over him. I can likewise see why men might feel a little insecure around him. He was everything a man is supposed to be . . . sexy, handsome, and he spoke as smoothly as satin.

Needless to say she melted and I will be grateful to Cary Grant for that kindness for the rest of my life. I can see why he and my father were so popular when they were younger. That level of style and smoothness ought to be illegal and he was getting up in years. It must have been downright impossible to have brought an eligible young woman around him when he was young and in his prime.

****

For a man who spent the majority of his life in the motion picture business, Randolph Scott had relatively few close friends from it. That's pretty amazing if you think about it. He spent close to thirty five years in league with the top-ten actors, but the number of friends he had acquired from all the films he made was only a small handful. Considering his reputation for genuineness and manners, I guess that's not really surprising. He knew, and was friendly with, a great number of individuals from a vast diversity of lifestyles and backgrounds, including the motion picture industry. They were all people of intelligence and possession of a strong character and moral convictions.

He had friends from the motion picture industry, it is true, and some we have discussed earlier. One of my favorites was my godmother, Donna Reed. She was a remarkable woman to have balanced life with her producer/husband, Tony Owen, their children and her hectic schedule on the set. Charming and lady-like at all times, she and my father had obviously known each other for a long time — even before each finally settled down to a husband and a wife and children. There was a nice magic between them. I saw it often as we grew up.

Donna's husband Tony Owen was the producer of her television series "The Donna Reed Show." Tony and Donna were nice people to be around when my sister and I were young. I was never very close to Donna's children so I spent little time with them. My visits with them came more as mandatory social obligations with my parents. There was a time when Tony took us out on his fishing boat. God, what a disaster that was! I was seasick for the whole trip. That's when I found out the smell of diesel engines was too much for me.

It's probably when I decided that I liked sailing over the thumping, stinky drone of powerboat engines. I found out one irritating fact about my father

Donna Reed was my godmother and a very good friend of the family.

on that trip, though. He never suffered from motion sickness or seasickness. He was telling the passengers of the boat how he had gone over to Europe when he was in the service in World War I on a troop ship.

He sat back in one of the fighting chairs on the afterdeck. He said that the men were stacked very tightly into those ships. "Boy, let me tell you. They loaded us in to those big troop carriers and packed us in like sardines. There must have been berths stacked five or six high." I remember he smiled for a moment. "Because of the number of men we rarely got to leave the interior of the ship. Most of the men with me were very sick. I was fortunate never to have had that problem."

That figures. Just listening to him talk made me sicker than I already was. I still have to fight the sensations of sea for the first day I am on the ocean and I have been sailing for the better part of thirty years.

When Tony Owen passed away and left Donna alone in the 1970s, Donna went through a long period of time with no male companionship. She later found someone who pleased her. I didn't know about it at the time, because I was living farther south in the San Pedro area of Los Angeles. My parents never were much for gossip about their friends, so I didn't know until I came up to attend my sister's wedding, which was held at our house. I met the man Donna married and found him to be a very pleasant individual who seemed to care a great deal for my godmother. He was a handsome man a few years her junior. His name was Colonel Grover Asmus, a former aid to General Bradley. Because of his work as a geologist on the Alaska pipeline, they lived for a number of years in Oregon. Ultimately they moved back to the house which Donna owned near my parents' house.

The day of my sister's wedding I heard a great deal of gossip floating around from many of the guests. When Donna arrived with her new husband in tow, many of the guests appeared to almost shun them. They were polite of course, but distant. It is my understanding that people not in the motion picture business tend to be a little shy around those who are, so that may explain at least some of the reticence which I observed that day. Not my father. He was all smiles and full of warmth as he greeted them.

I talked to him later that day and asked him his opinion of the situation. "Dad, what do you think about Donna's new husband?"

He just smiled and shook his head. "Oh, I don't know. He seems to make Donna very happy. It's not my business, but if he makes her happy then there is very little else to say." His concern was for Donna's happiness. Southern manners and Christian fellowship can be a marvelous gift. He could have cared less about the man's standing. His concern was for the happiness of his friend. That was a great attitude in my opinion, but what would you expect from a gentleman like Randolph Scott?

****

I have tried to keep my discussion of my father's friends limited to those men and women with whom most of you might be familiar thus far. All of the people I have mentioned so far are well known from old films or history books. They are colorful, famous and memorable from a number of different aspects. I think that makes them interesting to many of you who have not had the opportunity to have met them. There are a great number of others with whom my father associated himself who are not and were not as colorful. They were people who, while high ranking in their field or industry, are certainly not as well known or as colorful as some of the friends I have already covered.

Chief and foremost of these friends who were not associated with the motion picture industry and whose name will never be recorded in the history book was Frank Galvin. Frank was born in the East but my father began his association with him when he was managing the Beverly Hills branch of Security Pacific Bank. Frank is an unassuming man with an old style sense for business and finance. He and my father thought along the same lines in business. Both men worked very hard for the money they accrued and neither was quick to let it slide from their fingers. I know I have gotten that particular lecture from both of them.

Dad placed a great deal of trust in Frank's business savvy and moral principles. Frank was my father's most trusted advisor. Of course the two men played a great deal of golf together. I'm sure that many business ideas were formed out on the links. I know that because both men's minds could never stay far away from business, regardless of the surroundings. It was fascinating to watch them together. Raised in completely different backgrounds the men thought very much alike.

My father had a number of trusted advisors in business but none was so valued as Frank Galvin. Dad relied on Frank's sage counsel. As my father's health declined, Frank was of great help to my father in his business dealings. As a matter of fact, after my father passed away, Frank has become my mother's greatest advisor and confidant. His easy manner has made her transition from wife to executor of my father's estate much easier and less stressful than it otherwise could have been.

Frank, more than any other of my father's friends who were alive at the time of his death, has proven himself to be one of the finest friends for which one could ask. He helped my mother through the complicated paperwork and financial arrangements which are a function of the death of a loved one. He stood beside her and offered an incredible amount of moral support. Frank's dedication to my father and his extreme sensitivity to my mother have never wavered since my father's passing. He is always there for my mother should she need anything.

I greatly appreciate Frank Galvin's place in my parents' lives. He was a good friend to my father and has proven the best of friends to my mother. I haven't always gotten along with the man myself. He and I have butted heads over the years about a great number of issues. Actually they were the same issues with which I used to butt heads with my father. One thing is for sure: like my father, Frank has the innate capacity for differences in point of view. This may be one of the greatest similarities between the two men. They both were able to respect opposing views in discussions and situations placed before them without it affecting their demeanor and outlook into the problem with which they were dealing.

As I said Frank and I have not always gotten along, but I recall very well his comments to me after my father passed away. "Chris, if you need advice, please feel free to come to me anytime. I'm not always going to be agreeable but I'll help in whatever way is available to me." He has been true to that statement in the more than six years since my father passed away. Thanks, Frank.

****

My father passed away at the age of eighty-nine. In the later years of his life he watched a great number of his friends pass away before him. At times I think that must have been very hard to take. To live longer than your peers and the people with whom you grew up must be a tremendous burden. Yet, his life was rich in the number of friends and associates he garnered. He rubbed elbows with kings, statesmen, business giants and famous women. No wonder his mind was always working. It must be a very inspiring and a titillating existence to be as close to some of these people as he was. It kept his mind constantly fresh and challenged to have been able to meet with and discuss so many things with them.

I have only mentioned a few of the many people my father considered his friends. I haven't delved very far into their relationships because it was not the way my father believed friendships should be treated. He was, as I have said a few times in this book, a very private man. All that I have given you is the barest hint. The purpose of this book after all is to give you a little insight into the actor who was my father.

Randolph Scott met and knew a lot of people in his passage from life to death. Those who were numbered as his friends seemed to have a few things in common. They were all people of strong convictions and high moral fiber. Like him they were possessed and were consumed with doing the very best they could every day they lived. Life for them was a challenge which had to be met and overcome and surpassed. That philosophy makes a difference in your character if you truly take it to heart. They were also people of great experience in the world and had a thirst for knowledge. In that respect they were all great communicators. They spoke well for themselves. They were not arrogant about their past achievements but were always looking to the future for some new horizon to conquer.

I left out of this section a vast pool of friends with whom my father was close. These were people like Bob Hope, who needs no introduction; or Stan Hale, a high ranking executive with whom my father spent much of his time; and Clark Gable whose wife was a very good friend of my mother's. Of course, I would be remiss if I didn't mention Dinah Shore, who sang to me at my coming out party when my parents officially presented me to the world. Listed, too, was Howard Hughes who gave my father his first big break as an actor. His association with Hughes launched my father on a career which was rewarding but allowed him to touch the lives of millions of people across the country and around the world. His essence and his characters are still touching many lives through videos and reruns. All and all he had a good life. He amassed a bounty and a great wealth of people who still call him friend. In that way he will still be alive because he can't have truly passed on until there is no one left to remember him.

****

I almost completely forgot one of my father's most valued friends. I wish I had been older when he was alive. I think I would have appreciated him far more than I did as a child. I refer to my father's German Shepherd, Kurt. Boy, he loved that dog. It took Kurt a while to accept me when I was first brought home from the hospital. Once he figured out I was all right he was my constant companion and protector even during those times when I was outside in my playpen. I don't remember him very well but I can't imagine a better protector. From the pictures I have seen he was a big, big dog. My mother couldn't scold me when the dog was around. I was told he wouldn't let her. Now you know why a boy always loves his dog. From what I remember of my father's interaction with Kurt, I'd be willing to bet that he loved that dog to death.

Kurt died between my sixth and seventh birthdays. I don't remember much of what happened, but I do remember that the dog had severe arthritis for which he was taking medication on a daily basis. When Kurt finally became so crippled that he could no longer walk, I can recall Dad tenderly lifting the dog into his arms. Kurt was a huge Shepherd but my father lifted him easily. The one thing that struck me was that my dad was crying as he carried his friend to the car to take him to the vets. That was the first time I ever recall seeing my father cry.

It impresses me to this day that my dad was so very attached to that dog. To have reacted that way he must have loved that old German Shepherd very much. Maybe that is why I am so attached to my own animals. I can almost see my father and Kurt when the dog was only a few years old. Since he lived at the beach I can bet that they took long walks together. I'd also be willing to bet that my dad spent at least some of his time using Kurt as a silent confidant much as I do with my own dogs. I can relate to that although my father had a hard time relating to my ownership of dogs once I moved out on my own. Since he had always had a large yard he couldn't imagine that my dogs could be happy cooped up in small apartments. If he had only known just how well they adapted.

Here is Dad with Snowee, the Great Pyronese my mother bought.

No other dog ever took Kurt's place in my father's heart even though we always had dogs after Kurt. At the same time, none of the subsequent dogs was his choice. They were either my sister's and my choice or my mother's. Maybe he didn't feel that he could find another dog like Kurt, which is possible because Kurt was truly an amazing animal. I think he realized the importance of letting the family choose what most suited their needs. He was, after all, a very unselfish man when it came to his family.

In all fairness there was one other dog who managed to squirm into my father's heart. My mother purchased a large Great Pyranese. Snowee was a woolly and wonderful animal with a sweet disposition and an affinity for my father. I think with both my sister and I moved out by that time, my father gave her a portion of the affection and love he held for us, as we were not around all the time. When Snowee finally passed away, he cried for her departure from him.

Chapter 7

ON THE PRACTICAL SIDE

From the late 1940s through the 1950s Randolph Scott starred in some of the most popular outdoor action films. He was a consistent top box office hit for RKO, 20th Century Fox, Columbia, Paramount and Warner Bros. His films had a uniqueness about them that allowed them to do well in small towns as well as large cities. Exhibitors never failed to list his films among their top-grossing films, and his name was always at or near the top in the annual polls of actors and actresses whose names meant good business. In the motion picture business —even today — there is an expression that applied to Randolph Scott: "His name is money in the bank!"

It's too bad that Randolph Scott wasn't making films in the 1980s and 1990s and being paid at the current levels for top-draw performers. He'd have been much wealthier than he ever imagined. Since he was no longer making films by the time those years rolled around, he couldn't have realized the huge salaries and royalties which the top actors and actresses now garner. At the time my father made his films, the compensation for his work as an actor and his production value were much smaller than current levels. In fact the compensation was nowhere near what you might expect today. Couple that with the reality that taxes are not any where near as high as they were in the days when he was at his peak.

Compared to current levels, my father made very little money. Now we lived a more-or-less grand life style in contrast to many others, but it came less from my father's movie revenues than from his ability to make more money by investing his money wisely. As well as Randolph Scott did as an actor and a star, he was even more successful as a businessman. He chose to spend his money intelligently. His college education and his knowledge of finance allowed him to parlay whatever he made in films into a comfortable legacy for his family.

To be honest with you I'm amazed that he became an actor. He was always so level headed with his feet planted firmly on the ground. The movie business seems so much in the air. Acting is a glamour business but to my father it was a business. Certainly he studied acting and it paid off for him. Knowing my father I seriously doubt that he thought he would attain the status he achieved in his lifetime. In his mind there was never any room for "pie in the sky" or "pipe dreams" in his compelling desire for success. It was just a business in which he excelled. I don't think the glamour was important in his thinking or his dreams. It was just something to endure. If it had been important, he would have wrapped himself within it. He didn't. He was too level-headed and his feet were too well grounded to have let that aspect appeal to him.

His favorite comment to me was, "Don't count on the 'pie in the sky' dreams. The rewards you will ultimately gain will be from the solid well-thought-out work you do."

Now I may not know much about the movie industry but I know that it is as undependable as it can possibly get. Projects are conceived and paid for but sometimes are never produced. It might have been different in the earlier years of the industry, but somehow the unsureness was still widespread. He discouraged me from considering a career in films. He saw the changes which have run the gamut in the industry and even though there is a tremendous amount of money to be made, he didn't feel it was enough compensation for the effort.

"Son, there are so many people who want to be in acting. The hours are long and so often you have to be away from home. The industry has changed as well. It isn't the way it was back in the days when I started. I just wouldn't do it." He was right. It was more formal and the rules of behavior were established so that everyone knew what was expected.

Before I lay this next statement on paper I can already hear the environmentalists screaming. My father made the bulk of his wealth by being the non-operative end of his own oil company. He used to buy the mineral rights to what he thought were oil-rich properties. He and others would have test wells drilled. If they seemed like they would pay off, then other wells would be drilled. It's a nice way to make a living but that industry is far more complicated than it looks from the outside. The regulations are burdensome and they change at the whim and errant thought of each new political administration. Dad never shorted the rules or tried to find any loopholes. He believed in doing everything by the book even if it cost a healthy percentage more. He did and still managed to come out on top. There is not a large number of people who can make that boast and back it up.

Drilling for oil and natural gas seems to be a relatively simple business at first glance. I know that as a child I was fascinated by all the maps and the geological charts which littered my father's office in the George Elkins Building in Beverly Hills. (Ultimately he did move his office into the section of the house which used to belong to my sister and me. It was more convenient for him to be closer to his office as he approached his later years.) I loved looking at the maps on the walls with the colored pins stuck in them when I was young. Each represented wells in different stages. Some of the pins represented exploratory drilling sites, others were dry holes and yet others were producing wells.

It was a complex business. Which wells do you shut off and wait for the price to rise up and which wells do you hook up to what pipeline? It would drive me nuts. You had to hire geologists, drilling equipment, oil drilling teams and you had to obtain the necessary permits. There was never a guarantee that the well would be viable. If you had a good geologist you might have a small degree of certainty that the well you were digging might bear fruit or oil as the case may be. You had to know how far to drill down. At what depth do you call it a wash and pull out? If you found oil, how much oil was in the find, and how long would the well stay in production?

There are so many variables involved in that business and that is only the most apparent variables. Then there are insurances for a variety of different things, most of which are government-mandated as well as the moral mandates. All guided my father to one extent or the other in his endeavors in this industry. All of this and more had to be kept up to date in his books and records. It was a gigantic undertaking. I can't imagine anyone in their right mind choosing to take on a paperwork load of this magnitude, yet my father and his office staff of one felt very comfortable within those confines. In later years he did hire one more person to assist his secretary but that was many years after he first began the business.

****

Money, money, money! It seems that is all about which most people are concerned. It breaks up marriages and lifetime friendships. It drives close friends to the extreme of violence. We measure a person's worth by the amount of it or the number of things they have bought with it. When I attended the University of Southern California, the amount of money your parents had could be a determining factor as to whether you would be accepted into a given fraternity or sorority. I've had my share of problems with it and so have the people I have encountered and watched throughout the years. Everyone at some time or another is preoccupied with money.

Yes, even my father was obsessed with money but not as you might assume from his position in the community. Dad was very careful with his investments and also with the things he purchased. Waste was one of the issues which weighed heavily on him in his everyday dealings. He worked hard to provide an economically enriched environment for his family. He was not extravagant . . . not on himself, in any event, except when it came to his golf game.

Early golf photo of Pat and Randy Scott

He worried a lot about money in the respect that he was careful how he placed it. He was never one to foolishly or unintelligently toss money at a project without thorough investigation and research. Some people hear of an investment and immediately run down to the bank and take out their life savings to apply to it. Most of those schemes don't work. I'm sure that there were times when my father missed an occasional investment because he was meticulously thorough in his research of the investment and he found it hard to turn loose of his money. (It just occurred to me that my father was of Scottish descent. I've heard that the Scots were occasionally tight-fisted with their money, although frugal is more likely a better way of expressing it.) That might have made him too slow to take advantage of some opportunities. I think that thorough knowledge of the business playing field tends to make you less worried about where or what your money is doing.

All modesty aside I think we were wealthy . . . wealthy in a variety of ways, the least of which was money. Here, however, I am referring to monetary wealth. We lived in the nice part of Beverly Hills and we wanted for nothing reasonable. All through my school years we either rented or owned a cottage at one of the country clubs in Palm Desert. My father also kept a number of other memberships to other golf clubs. Why not, since golf was his chief recreation? All in all we lived a very comfortable and secure lifestyle. It wasn't extravagant although there are those who might call it that. It also wasn't elitist but there are those who will say that it most certainly was. What was it then? It was a modest reflection of my father's station and level of success. We were by no means ostentatious and we could afford the best of what was available. That doesn't mean that we spent money foolishly on the most expensive item available. It simply means that we had the capability to purchase the best if it was reasonable. Money was a tool to be used with respect and responsibility and not to be abused or taken for granted.

"Son, having money entails a responsibility." He would sigh when we had this discussion. "If you learn to live at a given level, and it is a level you can maintain, you won't have any problems. If you live below your means and you put money away, you will never go without in times of reversal. Anyone can live above their income. That is why I hardly ever borrow money. If I can't afford to buy it then I can do without it. The worst thing you can do is depend on credit to afford the things you want. You remember that."

I did and I do remember that lesson. I spent my time living above my means and I suffered for it. I heard that lecture a few times in my adulthood but he was right. The trick is to live within your means and not count on money you don't already have. (As a side note I should point out that when he passed away a number of my acquaintances commented that I was going to be wealthy. I didn't inherit my father's money, nor did my sister. The estate went to my mother which is where it should have gone. When she passes away — which I hope is a long time from now — my sister and I will inherit our share. A little might be nice but I don't think my lifestyle will change very much. I like the simple existence I have created for myself and I am not of the right disposition to move to someplace fancy and spend a lot of money. I guess my father taught me too well.)

He never patted himself on the back for the amount of money and property he amassed. They were the things that would provide security for the people he loved. I'm not sure it was a conscious thought but I'd be willing to bet that he wanted to make sure that his family would be secure after he was gone as well. He wasn't out to take away from others as some might. There was no percentage in pursuing a strategy like that. He simply, in a straight forward way and without denying others their due, put his money to work for him. Obviously he sent his money to the right places because it always came back to him in larger quantities than it left. That's the American way, after all, isn't it?

No get-rich-quick schemes or dubious investments to garner money. There were no commercials or endorsements for inflated paychecks. He didn't even cheat on his taxes. Since his accountant is my accountant, I can tell you that this is a man who never ever paid anything less than his fair share. Yes, I know that if you listen to the press you think that the wealthy never pay their fair share. That may be true in a great number of instances, but let me assure you that where it involved my father, he was too patriotic to have paid less than his share.

"Judas Priest."

I walked into my father's office one time when he was doing taxes at his desk. "What's the matter, Dad?"

My father looked up. "Just taxes, Son. I have to keep up with the laws. They just take so much. Sometimes it doesn't seem very fair that a man work so hard only to give it to the government."

Since I knew nothing of taxes and taxation I asked what I thought was an obvious question. "I thought that there were a lot of loopholes in the tax system." I asked that being quite naive about the laws governing taxes at that time.

My dad took off his glasses and laid them on the desk. No smile, just a serious business-like expression which he wore a good deal of the time when we had discussions of this nature. "You always have to pay your fair share. Those loopholes are for the people who want to cheat the government and I won't cheat." He was deadly serious about that, too. "If everyone paid their fair share, the tax rate would be much smaller." His eyes narrowed as he finished that statement.

****

What do we use money for? If you have a lot of money, on what would you spend it? How much of it would you spend on yourself? There was very little my father denied our family and more specifically my sister and me. I'm not speaking of extravagance here, not at the moment anyway. I am referring to the everyday needs and some of the necessary luxuries which accompany the area in which we lived. Those were never denied. We could afford those things with ease because of my father's monetary worth. I suppose I should have dressed better considering the funds which were available for clothing but I preferred blue jeans and shorts. Labels weren't important, just the fit. Of course, designer labels and names of clothing weren't important to my father, either.

For my mother and the kids there was almost nothing he wouldn't give us if it was within reason. When it came to himself, he was much more frugal. He liked clothes to fit well and last. To that end he used to have his suits made for him. He wasn't an elitist about it, but clothes off the rack just didn't fit as well as the hand made suits. Fashion certainly wasn't the issue either as my father had some suits that had been made for him thirty years before. He still wore them and they looked as if they had never been worn. He took care of his belongings. They were not considered disposable.

You would think with his prominence that he might have indulged himself in some luxury items. He liked American cars, I think, less for their quality but for the fact he believed in supporting American industry. He used to nag me from time to time about my always wanting to drive foreign cars. While my mother liked to drive Lincoln Continentals, my father preferred to drive Thunderbirds. You might think that they changed cars frequently as they could easily afford to do so, but they didn't. My mother bought a new car every four or five years. In the 1950s and part way through the 1960s, my father purchased a new Thunderbird every four years or so until he got his 1965 Thunderbird. He kept that car until he was no longer able to drive, which was just a few years before he passed away in 1987.

One of his friends who owned a car leasing agency in Beverly Hills tried for years to talk Dad into driving a car more befitting his station in life . . . something like a Mercedes-Benz. His friend spoke to him about it often enough so Dad tried it for about a week. It was a nice car but my father did so little driving (We lived less than four miles from his office in Beverly Hills.) that it hardly seemed worth the effort to spend so much money on a car. Dad certainly wasn't into showing off his station in life by driving a fancy over-priced foreign car. I guess that goes hand in hand with the conservative way in which he dressed. Looking at him and his clothes he didn't need to change anything. He always looked good.

He used to tell me that you didn't have to be flashy to be noticed. I have always enjoyed a certain . . . flair in my clothing that my father didn't really appreciate. He dressed very conservatively and he looked good in his clothes. He tried his best to educate me as well as he could about lasting styles and fashions.

I remember the discussions. "Son, you look so good in a suit. Why do you always have to go out looking so casual?" That was his polite way of asking why I always looked like I was going to the beach.

He smiled knowingly at me. "You know, you're a big man. You don't have to wear all those flashy clothes to get attention. Leave those to another man. A man like you will be recognized wherever you go. As tall and as well built as you are, you are always going to stand out in a crowd." He meant that in both the way I dressed and the kind of cars that I drove. I will have to admit that there was a time in my life when I liked driving Porsches and Mercedes but those days have long passed. Since my early thirties I have relegated myself to the lower profile of a Subaru station wagon or other similar vehicle.

In my clothing, however, I have diverged greatly from the path toward which my father tried to guide me. Dad loved his understated clothing. It suited his image and his personality. His conservative suits and plain shirts looked good on him. He didn't need to dress differently because his gentlemanly manner and rugged good looks set him apart. His manners and size always made him stand out in a crowd. Plus my father was raised in a more formal era. He dressed for dinner as many people of his age did. It was expected when they were younger. They carried the tradition with them through life. It was only rarely at our house that my father did not have on at least a sports jacket. It was a part of his personality. When he was dressed, he looked comfortable.

I just couldn't conform. Spending time at the beach and sailing have thrust me into a little more obvious mode of dress. Hawaiian shirts and shorts have been the rule of the day for me. My mother and he tried their very best to teach me the right way to dress when I was younger; but all it served to make me do was to hate getting dressed up. Fortunately, I do remember some of it so that on the rare occasions when I do get dressed to the nines, I do it with a modicum of the conservative style I was given as a child.

****

More often than not people think that because you have money you spend a lot of money. I guess sometimes it seems that way. To my father money was the means to an end. He didn't spend it frivolously. Take for example the house where I was raised. We moved into that house within a few weeks of my birth. The very first time that my mother felt the need to tamper with the house and its look was in the mid-sixties. The house was fifteen years old at that stage. None of the carpet or the upholstery had been changed in all that time.

I can see my father just shaking his head as my mother decided what was going to happen to her room, my father's room, the living room and the lanai. It was beyond him. There were fabric swatches and carpet samples strewn all over the house as my mother narrowed down the choices for the various rooms. No one was safe if my mother was in a given room, especially my father.

My mother would notice him walking by. She most often at that time had samples in front of her. "Randy. What do you think about this fabric for the chairs?" My mother would look up at him.

My father fingered the sample fabrics looking very serious. "They all look good to me, Pat. You choose whichever one you think is best." He didn't care. My mother has exquisite taste in decorating. He knew that regardless of the choices the house would look good.

The money had to be spent if the job was to be done right but he was resistant to let go so much of it all at one time. Still he gave my mother whatever she felt necessary to fulfill her vision of what she wanted the inside of the house to look like. To describe all that my mother accomplished would take a book in and of itself. Suffice it to say that she did a beautiful job. Even though just decorated, the house didn't ever look sterile or lacking in warmth. That was because of my mother. She made the house into a home.

I had always liked my father's room, but after she finished decorating it was better by a few fold. Originally that room was very dark. It had a dark carpet and heavy dark drapes. When she finished it was much lighter and airy, but still looked very masculine for my father's comfort. I loved the carpet. It was so plush and warm looking. It was a bone or sand base with streaks of brown and beige running through it. It is more appealing than I am making it sound. As the light of the day changed, so too did the texture and highlights of the carpet. If I could afford that particular carpet, I would have it in my office too.

I recall talking to my father in his room when he was paying the bill for that carpeting. I accidentally looked over his shoulder at the bill. I damn near died. "Oh my God! Is that how much you paid for this carpet?"

My father turned and looked at me over his reading glasses. A smile twitched onto his lips. "It is rather criminal to pay that much for a piece of carpet but it will be worth it or so your mother tells me." He chuckled a little as he joked.

I stared at him open-mouthed and slack-jawed. "How?"

My father removed his glasses, laying them on the desk. "If you buy the best you very rarely have to replace it. If this carpet lasts for twenty years, I will have spent less for it than if I had bought a lesser grade and had to replace it every few years."

He was correct as always. That carpet is still on the floor in his room and it still looks as good as the day it was laid. His attitude was to buy it right the first time.

If you can afford it, that is a great attitude. It was an intelligent approach, but it was one that you had to be able to afford to maintain.

****

I won't leave this section without admitting that there was one area in which my father indulged himself. He played golf and he allowed himself a slight indulgence where that was concerned. Now I have met some wealthy people in my time who also played golf, and it was nothing for them to travel around the United States and play at the most famous and highly-touted clubs. These people stayed at the finest hotels and ate at the fanciest restaurants. My father wasn't like that. He may have felt like doing that on rare occasions, but his needs were simpler and his sense of appropriate expense left no room for such overt frivolities.

Dad liked to stay as close to home as his shooting schedule permitted, so golf was a sport he practiced close to home. He did spend a little money in belonging to what he considered the finest country clubs. His idea of the finest were clubs whose greens staff kept the fairways well groomed and the greens smooth and lacking in blemishes. When I was young, he belonged to the Bel-Air Country Club that was deep in the heart of Bel-Air, a hilly suburb which was due west of Beverly Hills.

I liked that club. Maybe not the club exactly, but the drive to the club. I remember driving up the winding roads that led to the club house with my father in his old 1955 T-Bird. Those were good days. Once a month my father would take me to the barber shop at that club to get my haircut. He felt it important to present a neat clean-cut appearance at all times, so he and I would get our haircuts at the same time.

He kept the membership in the Bel-Air Country Club until the 1960s when he was awarded a membership in the Los Angeles Country Club. The Los Angeles Country Club was one of the most exclusive clubs on the West Coast. It was definitely one of those elite clubs which screened its prospective members very well. One criteria to which they adhered very strongly was that they didn't want any actors. My father was the exception — they admitted him. I'm sure that a great deal of debate went into that decision.

I never questioned my father about how they managed to put aside one of their primary rules but I think I have a pretty good idea. Of course, at the time my father joined, he had retired from the movie industry. By that time he no longer was involved in making movies and he was already well established as a businessman. His reputation for being a gentleman and his unassuming manner were legendary. Many people thought very highly of my father including some of the members of the L. A. Country Club. I'm positive that it was their influence and testimony as to my father's character that gained him admittance to the club.

He paid for that membership as did anyone else who was permitted to join. Dad would never have been tacky enough to discuss the expense of joining and maintaining his membership at that club, but all you have to do is look around that club to know that the cost of keeping it in perfect condition meant that the members paid a high price. It was one of his few extravagances and it was well worth the price for him. Besides it was close to the house. Still it was worth the price for him. Many of his non-movie business cronies belonged to the club and best of all the Los Angeles Country Club offered two separate courses — the North Course and the South Course. The North Course was the most difficult and the longest of the two courses. It was a challenge for the best golfers. Also the third green and the fourth tee were separated from our back yard by only a chain-link fence. Dad liked to play this course, but as the years progressed, he was relegated more and more to the South Course because it presented a less demanding walk and a slightly reduced degree of difficulty. I used to tease him about his playing the "old man's course". That never bothered him because at least he was playing and that, after all, was the point of belonging to the club.

I cannot recall when we started going to Palm Desert for vacations and school holidays but I'm sure we started going as a function of my father's need to get away from town and yet not be far away from his favorite recreation. Before the Eldorado Country Club was built in the 1960s, we used to go to the Thunderbird Country Club. Both were nice clubs but the Eldorado Country Club was by far and away the nicer. Of course, it was newer and it covered a much larger area. It was designed with a greater membership in mind and was a function of the needs of those golfers who visited the area on a regular basis, reflecting their needs better than other clubs that had been established long before.

As I look back to that time I begin to understand. It was like a smorgasbord for the golfer. By the time I was in my middle teens there were more than six or seven country clubs within a ten or fifteen mile radius. For my father that must have been a little like heaven. He belonged to several clubs in those days. That must have given him a great feeling to know that he could choose more than one course on which to play. I think he preferred the Eldorado but he did, on occasion, play at some of the other courses in the area.

The price of membership was never the issue. It went

without saying that he could afford that and a great deal more. The memberships in the various clubs allowed him the freedom to pursue his one true passion with the sport of golf without taking him far away from his family. His indulgence in his game allowed my sister and me to have a place to go where we could be with our friends. It gave my mother a social atmosphere where she could meet with her friends. All in all my father spent his money wisely and he never discounted the happiness of his family in the process of doing what he loved best.

He had the best golf clubs. They were custom-made for him which isn't unusual in itself considering his height and specific needs from a set of clubs. They were no doubt expensive, but I don't think he had more than one or two sets in the entire time I have been alive. (I have the putter he used since I was a child in my own golf bag. He used that putter as far back as I can recall and although he from time to time used others, he always returned to using that one special putter. For me it's not the best putter I ever used but when I play it is like having a little piece of my father with me.) He bought his golf balls over the counter. It never would have crossed his mind to spend the extra money to have them personalized with his signature, although I know that on a few occasions people gave that kind of ball to him. He rarely used them unless they were the brand he customarily used. Over all he spent very little in the pursuit of his passion other than the initial investment of his golf clubs and the yearly dues to the country clubs where he belonged.

As my friends and I developed an interest in golf and the skills to play it in a half decent way, we cultivated an attitude about the game. One was: golf carts were cool. The problem was my father never used golf carts. To his way of thinking it detracted from the game. He played to be in the sunshine and to get a little exercise. Until I fully understood his feelings and saw his reasoning I felt mortified when playing a round of golf with him, especially if I saw some of my friends. The golf cart that the family owned in the desert was more for my mother's use than for his use on the course. Even if he did use a cart, he would let others use it while he chose his club and walked to his ball.

Realistically he spent very little on himself in a monetary

sense. He was quite satisfied in using his money to provide security, pleasure and happiness for his family. Time was the real expenditure he gave to himself but only after he had fulfilled his obligations of time spent with his family. Others could not have been as giving of their time as my father. There may also have been times when he might have regretted having given so much, but I kind of doubt it. Responsibilities were that way and golf was the reward he treated himself to when all was said and done. He shared his reward with me as time in both our schedules permitted. It was great fun to be on the course with my father. I just wish he would have missed a shot occasionally.

****

There is family . . . close immediate and related to you in some fashion. Then, there is the extended family that usually includes friends of varying degrees of closeness and this is certainly true when considering my father, my family and the only two secretaries I can recall who worked for my father. I was born in 1950 which means that I barely recall the first who left my father's employ in the early 1960s. The next secretary I remember is Miriam and she is still working for my mother as I write this in October of 1993.

My observation is that Miriam never has been just an employee. She is an integral part of the family. She shares in the family and in all the events, trials and successes to be found within those bounds. To me she has been more like an aunt. To my father I think she was part sister, part employee, part organizer, part confidant and part advisor. Her loyalty to the family has extended far beyond that of a close worker and into the level of family member . . . a close family member. I guess it was only natural that this happened, as Dad treated her as an equal and over time valued her in his behavior as a member of the family.

I feel that both of my parents did that same kind of thing to all the people who worked for them over the years — whether they were housekeepers or nannies or Leng, the man who was my father's right-hand-man around the house. Leng is a unique story in and of himself. He was with my father longer than he was married to my mother until the year of his death. Leng was so much of a part of the family that he tended to be very jealous of the kitchen and how it was organized. For the longest time he did the marketing and the shopping. My parents chose the menu within limits and it was Leng's job to make sure that it was carried through.

Closeness can at times make it hard on relationships when they are family or otherwise. More than a few times my mother and Leng found themselves on opposite sides of an issue relating to the meals or the kitchen. Dad would stand the middle ground and ease the feelings on both sides. I think it might have been hard for him to have lost either one as both were part and parcel of the core family. In a few instances it seemed to me that one or the other would have to break but that Southern slyness of my dad's always averted the crises whatever the nature.

I liked Leng and he loved my sister and me. There was nothing he wouldn't have done for us. In my father's absence he advised us and took care of us. Leng was part-time mother, father and uncle all the years we lived in the house. The duty that fell to him was the running of the household which he felt should run smoothly and efficiently. The care and the well-being of all who resided in the Scott household were his familial responsibility. He was a great arbitrator in his own right as well. He ran interference more than once for me and at least a few times for my sister as well.

You might think that as a live-in employee he might well have overstepped his bounds as close to the family as he was. He did and he knew it. Still he was a part of the Scott family. We would have been poorer without his sage advice and thoughtful interferences. I never saw much of my father's family, as they lived on the other side of the country from us, but surely none of those people could have been closer to my father than was Leng. I watched them very closely. When I was young and on those rare occasions when it was just the two of them sitting or standing alone, they didn't act like anything more or less than good friends or brothers.

As I grew up, Leng was an extension of my dad. When my

Leng pictured in the living room of the Scott house in Beverly Hills

father couldn't be there — or when he was unavailable — it was Leng to whom I turned for advice and counseling. I didn't notice it that much when I was at home but as I aged I compared the principles and philosophies and found that both espoused the same thing. Not with the same words, but in substance they both believed the same way. This may have been one of the reasons they were as close as they appeared. Whatever the reason, having Leng around as I grew up and matured, was like having a second father about and that made me feel very special indeed.

Leng would come to me if I were doing something wrong. "Christopher, your father would be very disappointed in you if he knew you were doing that. You do something different." He would chastise me.

There were times when my father would express his feelings to Leng because he was having some difficulty in telling me. I think talking to Leng helped him focus his thoughts and possibly gave him a different slant on the problem he was having with me.

I remember a time when I was visiting my parents' home. I had been living on my own for several years and Leng came to me while I sat in the kitchen drinking a soda. He sat down in the chair across from me and put his right hand on my left arm. "You know, Christopher, your father is very proud of you."

I shook my head. "I'm not so sure, Leng."

Leng laughed. "Leng no give you bull shit. Your father talk about you all the time. You just remember the lesson he taught you."

****

It may come as no surprise to those who knew my father that he was a staunch conservative. I mentioned that Dad's business practices were more or less conservative as he preferred thoughtful investment over slick-sounding, quick-return schemes. So, too, were his politics conservative. I guess that may come as no great surprise as he was friends with Dwight Eisenhower and Richard Nixon. As a matter of fact, if you were to visit my mother's house you would find an old framed photograph of my father and Dick Nixon. Beside it is the score card that verifies that Richard Nixon shot a hole in one.

It was popular in those days to be of conservative views and values. Those principles and ideals seem to be equated in the 1990s in less than complimentary terms by far too many people. I don't think my father would have agreed. He might smile knowingly and nod his head if you wanted to chastise him for his views, but it would never sway him from what he believed was right and true. His beliefs were the product of a lifetime of service to his fans and to his country. He firmly believed that, right or wrong, the United States was his country.

He was ashamed of the doom and gloom liberals of the 1960s who burned the American flag and destroyed their draft cards. He fought in World War I and did his part with the USO in the second world war. It was his duty and he performed it without question. He was, after all, reared an American in the turn of the century South that I'm told is one of the most patriotic sections of the country. He believed that one of the principles which made this country what it is, was the ability of its citizenry to voice their disenchantment. He felt that it was a privilege to be able to vote and I cannot recall a single time that he failed to exercise that privilege.

He saw the value of change through the Democratic process. It must be so for the country to survive. Certainly he disagreed with the policies of various elected officials and he voted his disapproval. Yes, at times he spoke out against legislation but he obeyed the laws as they were written, not as he might have liked them to be. He knew the system was less than perfect, but he believed it was up to the people to more closely approximate the perfection inherent in our country's concepts and the few parchments that were left us by the men and women who founded this country.

He didn't have to agree, much less believe in, an ideology to have stood fully behind the right of a person to voice it. He disdained taxes, especially at the levels he had to pay for most of his professional life. Throughout much of his career in the motion picture industry, he paid well over fifty percent of his income. Still, he paid his fair share when many around him did not. For him there was never any question about it. It would have been unforgivable for him to stoop to fancy diversions for his money to avoid paying his fair share. Don't get me wrong, he sheltered some of his money in well-established legitimate ways, but they were always clearly within the bounds of the law. There was no bending or stretching of the laws for his gain. That is why he always ended up paying such a large percentage of his income to taxes. It would have been against his principles to have done any less. (As an aside, Randolph Scott never ran contrary to his principles.)

****

I had marveled at my father as I grew up and throughout all but the last few years of his life when the ravages of age finally caught up with him. He had always, and I do mean always, looked so well and fit. His waistline was trim and his muscle tone was excellent considering his age. Some of it was certainly genetic but there were other components, those being regular exercise and a proper diet.

The diet part for him was easy. We had cooks who worked for us whose job was to keep us well fed. We didn't eat extravagantly in the sense of fancy cuisine and heavy sauces. We ate well-balanced and well-prepared meals. My parents weren't into the more chic styles of eating. Actually, it's too bad they didn't want to venture out of that eating rut. Some of the cooks whom they employed were capable of many assorted culinary masterpieces. The rule of the day was: just keep it simple and cook it properly.

I guess I should feel jaded having grown up in a household which employed cooks and domestics. I don't, although there are times when I miss seeing some of the more memorable characters who worked for the family through the years. Dad never hired any illegal aliens. Most of the people he hired, with the exception of cooks, usually worked for us until they were too old to work.

That's off the subject so let me get back to the topic. The other daily routine which kept my father healthy was exercise. He did a fifteen- or twenty-minute set of exercises every

Randolph Scott in his late seventies, visiting Sandra in Boulder, Colorado

morning. Nothing elaborate — it was just a series of push-ups, sit-ups, chin-ups and mild stretching. Nothing was started by my father until he had done his exercises.

I would sometimes walk in to hurry him along, especially if I needed to do something with him. He would be in the middle of his routine. "Come on, Dad. What's taking you so long?"

My father would smile as he did his sit-ups. "I'll be with you in a few minutes, Son." He never broke his pace or lost his concentration regardless of the suddenness of my appearance.

I waited patiently for him to finish. One time as he was finishing, I asked him why. "How come you do this every morning?"

There was a sly smile on his face as he answered. "As you grow older, Son, you will see the value of what I am going to tell you. It is very important to be regular, not just in doing the exercise as I do, but, in every aspect of your life."

I was puzzled. "What do you mean by regular?"

"I mean taking care of yourself. God only gives you the one body and it is your responsibility to take care of it. You have to brush your teeth after meals. You have to eat smart. I have to do these exercises every day to keep fit and I use the military brushes on my hair to keep my scalp healthy." He chuckled. "You also have to approach life in moderation. You shouldn't eat too much nor should you drink too much." He was being cute with the last comment. There was feeling and conviction in his words but he was grinning while he spoke them.

I looked up at him. "Do you really think that's true? I mean, I have seen you sit down and eat a full meal and then turn around and eat a huge piece of chocolate cake. The thing that irritates me is that you never seem to gain any weight."

This statement got him laughing. "Son, I'm just one of the lucky ones. I can afford to indulge myself from time to time and it doesn't show. I've spent all my life taking things in moderation."

"Yeah, I know. If I even look at a piece of cake I gain weight and I exercise more than you." That was one of the things that irritated me about him.

"Practice moderation in your diet a little more and you won't have that problem." He patted my stomach. "If you do that, you won't have to worry very much about gaining." He chuckled. He was really annoying in a half-serious way. He was trying to get his point across without having to beat me on the head with it.

****

Practical is one thing. So, too, is moderation. Wastefulness is tantamount to throwing money away. My father hated waste of any kind. How long will you use a pencil? Me — I discard a pencil after it is about one third its original length. My father saved them and used them until they were all but point and eraser. He just couldn't get past seeing the silliness of throwing it away if it was still usable.

The first couch I remember in our house must have had down pillows because we were always pulling feathers out of the fabric of the cushions. My father instructed us to give him all of those feathers as they came out of the furniture. When we gave them to him he would put them in a small box in the projection room that was behind one wall in the living room.

I couldn't have been more than a few years old when the sense of this act nagged at me. I had found one of the down feathers. I walked up to my father who was sitting in his favorite chair reading the paper. I extended my chubby child's hand to him with the feather in it. "Here."

My father looked at me and smiled. "Thank you, Christopher." He rose from his chair and walked to the projection room where he pulled the box down from the second shelf. That shelf was just beyond my reach so it was safe there.

I watched him curiously. "What are you going to do with them?" I stared at him inquisitively.

He smiled down from the sky at me. "I'm going to save enough to make you a pillow."

I know I smiled widely. "Really? A pillow? For me?" I thought for a moment. "When?"

I think my father laughed at my inquisitiveness. "Just as soon as the box is full."

I nodded my head and started to walk back into the living

room. I didn't understand so I turned back while my father was closing up the box. "When's that?"

Dad laughed again patting me on the head. "Soon." He must have gotten a charge out of my inquisitiveness because I can recall him laughing or chuckling frequently when I was young.

What a terrible response. To a small child soon can be tomorrow or next year or a lifetime away. It was no use to question him further as it would have done me no good, for he had his point. Why throw it away if it has some usable function? I guess that is true because I still have the pillow he had made from all of those feathers.

****

Practicality was a true part of my father's personality as was integrity, moderation and intelligence. One thing which was practical was success. The steps to success in business and relationships were as simple as doing just a bit more than was required for the job. It was an integral part of his philosophy. It earned him respect, but more important was that by going the extra mile it gave him greater sense of self and of accomplishment.

I remember the day he felt it was the time to discuss his philosophy of going the extra mile. I was in my early twenties. Because I lived in San Diego at that time, I visited as often as was practical — that was once every few weeks. This was one of those times. We had been talking in the living room when he got up from his chair and started walking to his room. "Come with me for a minute, Son. There is something I want to give you." He walked down the short steps which lead to the solarium and his bedroom.

Curious I followed him into his room. I watched him as he sorted through a stack of papers that were on the top of his desk.

Finding a small soft-bound book he turned to me. He stretched out his hand with the small book in it. "I want you to read this at your convenience. I think you will find the message will be of benefit to you." He smiled slightly as I took it from his hand.

The book only had twenty or thirty pages in it. I thumbed through it looking at the small print which covered the pages. "What's this for?"

Dad smiled. It was the sort of sly smile you would expect from him. He already knew how I would react to the material he had asked me to read. "You just read it and see if that doesn't explain it."

I nodded my head and looked at the title on the nondescript booklet. The title read *Going the Extra Mile*. I don't recall the name of the author but it gave examples of people who succeeded by going further than was expected of them. I took the book home and read it through that night. I never discussed the book with my father but I took the message inside and ultimately put it into practice in my life. I hate to be corny but it has really made a difference in my life.

It was a simple premise. By doing more the chances that good things in life will swing your way is more probable. I think that is true. I got promotions and business opportunities that would never have come my way if I hadn't been willing to do more than I had to in a given instance. Not just that, but not to expect any special attention for doing it. The sense of that took a bit of time to sink in, but it did eventually. It was in the attitude. Going the extra mile was something you did for yourself, your internal sense of pride, and not for someone else.

After I read the book I began to take notice of how my father went about his duties and responsibilities. He did more than was expected. If someone thanked him for it and returned his actions in kind he seemed genuinely surprised. And why not? He hadn't gone the extra mile for that person. He did it as a matter of pride in himself . . . not for acknowledgment but because he was capable and took the time to do it. No wonder people always were so eager and willing to do things for my father! It was the way he treated them because of the respect he had inside for himself. If he had only done what was expected of him, I doubt that he would have been the giant he was.

****

Moderation and regularity were the keys. Practice fell into that category. It was almost a philosophy for him. It was practiced in all facets of his life. It was applied to his family, his business, his health and his golf game. It was the structure of his life. Time had taught him that to be overly indulgent was something to be avoided. He had a very keen insight into his own mind and needs.

I cannot leave this section without stressing just how practical my father was. It was his outlook. People who can be that measured in their approach to life wind up stiff and rigid in their views and opinions, as well as being a bit detached from the rest of us who are less controlled. My father never was stiff, although with age certainly some of his opinions and his habits tended to become a bit more ingrained. Still, he remained mentally flexible and capable of adjusting his perspective as times changed. He was able to meet new challenges with an air of confidence that might well throw another of his age and experience for a loop. He was graceful in the way he moved through life, and I suspect that was the direct result of the practiced patience and moderation which he tried to teach me.

Chapter 8

Problems

I have stated quite clearly and emphatically throughout this whole book that there was no "Mommy Dearest"-like story to be told about my father and my family. That is true, but that doesn't mean that there were not any problems. No, not problems with my father but with me. I was different from the rest of the family. I had some relatively severe problems that caused my family some embarrassment and a great deal of concern about my capabilities. I'm not sure that I would have had the patience and the courage to have stayed so unwaveringly beside a child of mine if he had the same dispensation for trouble and problems.

I have to tell you that this is the shortest chapter in the whole book. In this chapter I will do my best to describe the problems I went through in a more-or-less brief way but more important was how my family, mainly my father, contended with them. From experience I can tell you that it isn't very easy to keep your patience and stand beside a child who has some dysfunctions the size and nature of mine. I have gotten past them with a great deal of effort from my mother and my father.

****

From the time I was very young, I had grand ideas. I saw the world in different ways. In those days my father was always trying to get me to understand that great things rarely happen to and for you if you do not take the time to invest in reasonable and potentially sound projects and have the patience to see them to completion. Clearly impetuous, I rushed through almost everything. This must have driven my father to distraction since he was so meticulous and methodical in his approach to everything.

I have to say that he tried to understand and teach me properly. He sat me down when I was in my early teens while I was working on a model. I had asked him if I could get another one. "Dad, would you take me down to the hobby store so I can get another model?"

My father eyed the incomplete model which sat on my desk. "Don't you think you should finish the one you have before we get another one?"

I looked up at him. "I will but I really want to get another one."

He shook his head. "I think we can wait until you finish this one." He started to walk out of the room.

I wasn't ready to accept that answer. "Why?" I was irritated as I frequently was when I did not get what I wanted.

My dad looked at me with a concerned expression on his face. "Christopher, you have got to learn to do one thing at a time. You will never be successful unless you learn to take each thing as it comes. If you jump around too much you won't finish anything and then what will you have accomplished?" He walked out of the room to let me contemplate his thoughts. It was a lesson. He wasn't arbitrary but he was firm in his refusal to indulge such a selfish and spoiled whim.

This is an extreme case and one which happened very rarely but it gives you a good idea. Since my father neither spoiled me or overindulged me, I don't want you to get the wrong idea. The principal of what I am saying is that I didn't stay focused long enough on any one thing to complete it. That's one of the problems I had with school. In later years I discovered that I might have been blessed (or cursed) with some level of Attention Deficit Disorder. Looking back on my childhood, I can tell you that the symptoms were there in abundance. In those days we were unfortunately not as enlightened or as well informed about mental dysfunctions as now, so I was treated as if I just had a hard time staying with certain tasks, and that was true.

My father was always trying to come up with things or devices to keep me focused. Some worked and others failed miserably. The point here is that he kept on trying to insure I would grow up normally and properly.

****

My father meant a great deal to me. I wanted desperately to please him, but at times I felt so inadequate. The things which I knew he wanted me to do well, I either couldn't do or couldn't see to completion. I created a series of fabrications to him and to my mother which for a short time would seem to please them. Unfortunately that lying also bled over into all aspects of my life. It caused, over the years, an untold amount of trouble and heartache for my family.

My dad did his level best to understand what it was that troubled me and caused me to behave as I did at times. He tried talking to me on so many different occasions to help me alter my path. "Chris, why do you tell stories like this?" The concern was so evident in his eyes. The disappointment in his voice was very strong.

I would look at the floor. I had disappointed my father once again. "I don't know, Dad. I didn't mean to." He would look at me with the disappointment of my behavior evident in his eyes and on his face. "I can't impress upon you enough how this will affect you in your later years." He wanted me to understand the ramifications of my actions. Also, he wanted to find a way to get me to change.

"What do you mean?"

"People will judge you all your life on your character and your integrity. If you are known to be a person who cannot tell the truth, or if you cannot be depended upon; then the kind of people that you want to be around will avoid you like the plague."

Ultimately I found a way out of the problems that vexed me, but much of what my father told me came true. There were a number of people who avoided me because of my behavior and honestly I don't blame them. I overcame those problems close to a decade ago. Still, I had to go through a lot before I finally got the help I needed. My father was always there for me, even though I know that through the years some of my antics and behaviors hurt him.

****

It is hard as a male child to never have the chance or the capability of achieving the same stature or prominence as your father. This was certainly true in my case. Growing up with someone of Randolph Scott's stature and fame is difficult. It, of course, was not his fault. He was simply who he was. The problem was mine. How can I measure up in his eyes? What can I possibly do to be noteworthy in his eyes, considering what he has done and accomplished in his life? Those questions played at me and vexed me a good portion of my life. There was no logical reason for that feeling, I have to tell you. He never expected or required it from me, but inside I felt it. It was a self-inflicted stress that I laid upon myself. The burden that it instilled in me was incredible.

A number of different psychological dysfunctions can be brought about or activated by stress, whether it be real or imagined. In my case, it was imagined stress. That didn't make it any less real or painful to me. I think my father saw some of this coming. I'm not really sure, but I know that he tried his best to explain to me that I didn't need to be anything more spectacular than myself for him to be proud of me.

"Son, you don't have to be anything special to be the best in my book. You just be all that you can be and in whatever endeavor and I can assure you that I will be proud of you." The reality of his thoughts was that, just by being his son. I was special.

"I understand, Dad."

My father would shake his head. "No, I don't think you understand how much I want the best for you, Chris. It isn't important what you aspire to as long as it is what is inside of you."

He truly meant what he said to me in this regard. It really didn't matter to him what I did as long as it stayed within the guidelines he had taught me through the years and those guidelines were wide. They could encompass anything that I could have wanted.

I did well at most things; but occasionally as I matured, I took a flyer. All my plans would crumble in those instances. I expected that my father would have wanted to disown me but he never did. He was always there to help me pick up the pieces and try to get me back on the right track. His support never wavered although I know he felt I should have learned my lessons. Still family came first and I was his son. There was nothing he wouldn't have done for me to keep me on the right path and from setting the wrong course.

****

Most of my life I was as normal as anyone else, but there were times when some mental switch would click on in my head and I then would act strangely or out of character. The problems were less a function of what I was thinking than a product of the disorder which was a part of me. There were two times in my life when I had the opportunity to get help and both times when I reached out, it was my parents who were there to help me through it. I know it must have been hard on my father. He was born before the turn of the century and raised in a time when you didn't discuss mental disorders or dysfunctions. As I have said earlier in this book, he was more than capable of adapting to the changes that went on in the world and of adjusting his thinking.

When I was twenty-seven years old, I lived in a triplex in San Pedro very close to the water. Because it was built on a hill, my apartment had a view of the ocean that was phenomenal. I was sitting in my apartment looking out over the water of the Pacific Ocean. I can't explain why, but many of the things I had done wrong in my life flooded over me like a massive tidal wave.

I picked up the phone and called my mother. I told her what had happened to me. "Mom, I think I need some help."

My mother responded from the other end of the line. "Don't

go anywhere. I'll find the name of a doctor and I'll call you right back."

I must not have waited more than ten minutes but it seemed more like an eternity at that time when the phone rang. It was my father. "Son, are you all right?" I could hear the concern in his voice. Even over the phone line it was very pronounced.

"I don't think so, Dad." My voice was breaking and I was shaking.

"Listen, Son, your mother has found a doctor at UCLA who will see you right away. I'll meet you there."

I hung up the phone and drove to UCLA. My parents met me at the Medical Center.

When I walked up to my father he put his arm around me. "Chris, I know that this is hard, but when you see the doctor you have to do all that he tells you to do. I'll be here if there is anything you need."

I felt better but I was scared. "Thanks, Dad. I really appreciate the support."

The psychiatrist gave me a battery of tests to determine my psychological profile. When it was all said and done he told me that there was a good chance that I was manic-depressive. Terrific. That was just what I needed to hear. I was mentally ill. The doctor gave me the names of several good psychiatrists who would be closer for me to see than he was. He told me to talk to them first to see which one would be most compatible to my personality.

Well, that summed it up in a nutshell. There was a reason for the odd behavior to which I had I succumbed on many occasions. Now all I had to do was to get some help for it. I started going to one of the doctors on the list. I saw him for a while but tapered off as the manic-depression came and went. That's the problem with that particular malady. It isn't something that is evident all the time . . . just some of the time.

Through all of it, my father was steadfast in his support of me. It could not have been that easy for him either. Even though he understood little of what my problem really was, he encouraged me to go to the doctor. "Son, you have got to treat this as if it were any other kind of illness. If you don't get the necessary treatments, you will not be completely free of the disease."

He also spoke at length with my doctor. He tried to keep me going, but after a few years I stopped going. My problem seemed to be under control. I was okay for a while but eventually, as with any untreated disorder, it came back. Manic-depression is a chemical imbalance which causes a person to behave in ways which can be contrary to his best interest. It needs to be treated both by drug intervention and therapy. I know it hurt my father although he said nothing about it to me, but it showed in his eyes. Maybe it isn't worth mentioning, but for the most part I was successful in my own enterprises, although not nearly as much as I might have liked to be. The few times that the manic-depression affected me served mainly to keep me from extending my successes. That is the way of manic-depression. It encourages you to do many things which are contrary to your best interest. It is insidious in that it isn't always working on you. There are times when you appear completely normal and behave as you really are. In the manic phase there is nothing you can't do — even if you can't — and therein lies the real problem.

****

I think that a great number of people with psychological problems fail to get help because they lack the courage to face the problem and themselves. I stated that I was given two opportunities to get help for my problems. The first I described in the earlier section. The second began the day I went to visit my father in the hospital in 1986. He was not doing very well. I sat in his hospital room and talked to him.

"Hi, Dad. How are you doing?" I looked at him. He was gaunt and thin. It depressed me to see him in that manner. This was no longer the rugged man who was my father. The image I had of him in my mind was six-foot-four and one hundred-eighty pounds and not the very frail man in the hospital bed who was in front of me.

He appeared weak as he turned to me. His body looked so frail in contrast to the way I have always seen him in my mind. You could still see the fires of determination in his eyes. "I've been better , Son. If I can just get these doctors to let me out of here." He looked up at me. "How are you doing?" I think he wanted to hear something other than what I was going to say.

I smiled putting aside the problems through which I was going. "Everything is just fine."

He looked through me with his steely eyes. "I hope so, Son. I'll know when you've finally learned." I felt as if a cold steel knife had been thrust into my heart and twisted as his eyes pieced through my facade. I wish he had said something to me but it was my job to admit my problems and not his to point them out. He had taught me as much as he had been able in his time with me. Now it was my turn. It was up to me to take the lessons to heart and make something of them.

It was obvious that his health was failing rapidly. Still he had tremendous courage. His love for me was more important than the problems which tore at him. I hurt inside knowing that I had failed him. Or had I actually failed myself? That is what he had taught me after all. Do what you know is right. Well. I wasn't doing what was right and I knew it. I also wasn't taking responsibility for my own life either. I was allowing too much to dictate my actions. I certainly wasn't putting the lessons he had tried so hard to impart to me into play.

A few weeks later Ron Ashmore, a very good friend of mine, came to my house to express his displeasure with my behavior. The discussion was very heated at times. He was trying his best to paint an accurate picture of what my behavior was doing to me and those close to me. I was doing my best to defend myself and keep from facing the truth of his words. When he went to bed, I sat by myself in the dark and contemplated the length and breadth of my life. It was pretty pathetic. Ron was right. I had been a coward far too often in facing up to what needed to be done, and as a result my life was in a shambles. It was not irretrievable but something had to be done right away.

The next morning I called the psychiatrist who had attempted to treat me in the past and told him that I wanted to commit myself for psychiatric treatment. He agreed. With that call out of the way, I called my mother to inform her of my decision and my new awareness. She and I talked about it and decided that it would be better not to tell my father. In his weakened condition it might be too much for him to take.

I checked into the hospital the next day. Realistically I could have walked out of the hospital anytime I wanted. That fact doesn't take away the fear you feel inside that when the door closes you are there for real. After you check into the hospital it is locked behind you. I remembered all the courage I had seen in my father all those years of my life. At that moment I was determined to set a course which would reflect the ideals that he tried so hard to teach me.

In the hospital I learned a great deal about myself and my feelings of insecurity. I also learned how my low self esteem made me feel less than adequate because I tried to compare myself to my father. The hardest lesson was to stop using my father as a measuring stick to give value to my accomplishments. I had to learn to measure myself by my own accomplishments. They are not as grand as those of my father, but they are mine. I fought hard to win them. With that revelation came an inner sense of confidence which I had never had until then.

Another hard lesson was learning to face the truth about myself regardless of how painful or disturbing it might be. That's why it took me so long to get the help. I had to learn take responsibility for my actions and put it where it belonged . . . on my shoulders. It was not a burden for my family and my friends to take and carry for me. It was a tough fight to unlearn that particular thought pattern. It was an even harder battle to learn new schemes of coping. The old schemes were so easy and were ingrained so deeply in my personality. I did it in the hospital. With a supreme effort and a justifiable trust in the hospital staff, I unloaded a vast quantity of the garbage which held me back.

I left the hospital after staying for three weeks, although my therapy to relearn how to live continued for several more years. Manic-depression gives you some very poor coping strategies. These strategies have to be unlearned before you can resume a more-or-less normal life. My therapy also included an eighteen hundred milligram Lithium requirement which would give me the chance to chemically control my problem until I had progressed far enough in my therapy to be taken off of it. I can't tell you how much I hated the Lithium. It didn't alter my personality as I feared, but there was one possible side effect and that was it could become toxic in your system. Lovely thought isn't it? It makes you wonder if the cure isn't possibly more dangerous than the disease. The real beauty of the Lithium is that it gives you a firm handle to grab in dealing with your aberrant behavior.

I left the hospital in late November of 1986. I saw my parents only briefly after the time of my release until that Christmas. When I arrived at the house, I was feeling very well. My mind and body were truly free for the first time in my life. I was strong inside for the first time since I don't know when. I spoke to my mother first before I poked my head in to see Dad. She and I discussed again whether or not I should tell him about what had happened. Because of his failing health, we both agreed that it would be best if nothing were said. Both my mother and I were fiercely protective of my father and his

Dad and me the Christmas before he passed away

health. He didn't need any disturbing news. The fact that I had been to a mental hospital might be considered disturbing, especially knowing how he was concerned about me and the problems which I had had.

We went out to the lanai to eat a pleasant Christmas dinner. It went well but things had changed for me. The changes and the way I felt about them made it very hard to keep my promise to myself and my mother with reference to talking about the hospital. After dinner the challenge not to speak became quite difficult.

Dad was seated in his favorite chair in the living room when the rest of the family exchanged gifts. It was odd the way he kept staring at me. I would look up from opening a package and his eyes would be scrutinizing me. "Christopher. Something is different about you. I can't put my finger on it but something in you has changed." I have stated a few times in this book that my father was extremely perceptive.

I looked up at him and smiled warmly, trying my very best not to show any emotion or trace of the revelations I had uncovered at the neuro-psychiatric hospital. "No, Dad. There's nothing different about me other than I grew my beard." I looked up at him. He was very thin and pale. He had lost a large amount of weight over the past year. I hated seeing him look that way. He looked older than I ever would have thought possible.

I have said that I could never get away with anything when dealing with my father. He didn't buy my comment and pressed the issue. "You can't fool me, Christopher. Something is different about you. Please tell me what it is." His eyes were clear and intense as they always were when he was searching my face for an answer.

I felt suddenly cold and empty about deciding not to tell him. What I had been through, what I had changed and what I had learned about myself threatened to come out. I bit my lip to answer him. "You're mistaken, Dad. There is absolutely nothing different about me." Too many years of never being able to fool him set up a very bad feeling in me. Here I was lying to him once again and he knew it. It was just like being between a rock and a hard place.

He continued to scrutinize my every move and the nuances of my voice until it was time for me to leave. I got up. "Well, I've got to go." I walked over to my dad and patted him on the shoulder and began to walk away.

He looked up at me and beckoned me back. "Doesn't your tired old father get a hug?" The intensity of his eyes and the fire behind them was brilliant.

I walked over to him and put my arms around his frail shoulders and gave him a hug. That close to him I could feel his eyes searching my heart and soul. "I love you, Dad. Merry Christmas." At that moment I wanted to tell him so badly that I was breaking inside.

He squeezed me tightly and whispered in my ear. "I love you, too, Son. Don't try to fool me. I know something has happened to you. I don't know what it is that has changed but it's apparent. Hopefully, you'll tell me soon." The strength of his need to know was overpowering. It radiated from him like a miniature sun.

I stood up and smiled at him. Inside I was sweating profusely. I really did want to tell him but I passed it off. "Well, maybe I will when I have something to say." I felt terrible not telling him. I wanted to jump up and thank him for teaching me to have the courage to face my problems but I still wasn't sure how he would react to it. In retrospect I should have known that it would have pleased him no end to have discovered that I was finally on the right track with my life.

As it was, I think he knew anyway. All my life it amazed me that he could see through me and into my heart and into my schemes. In spite of that ability, he was still my most fierce supporter and my best friend. I guess you can't ask for too much more than that.

****

The day before my father passed away, I went up to see him. He had lapsed into unconsciousness a day or two before. I sat with him in his room. I looked down at him lying so peacefully in his bed and I knew that he was fighting to stay alive. That was his way. Life was a precious gift and he was fighting to keep it. The sad thing is that I believe that he wasn't trying to stay alive for himself. He was fighting to stay alive because of his family. He had been protector, provider and friend to all three of us. Even in this fight to keep living I think that was his motivating thought.

He wouldn't quit until he knew that everything was going to be all right. He looked terrible. He had lost so much weight. It pained me to see him that way. Was he hanging around to make sure that everyone was taken care of? Looking at him I knew what I had to do. In my own way I had to give him the peace of mind that I was at least squared away. I knew he was unconscious but maybe the feelings of my message might reach him.

I squeezed his hand and spoke to him. "Dad, I want you to know that you were right last Christmas. There is something different about me. I went into the neuro-psychiatric hospital last year. I'm not completely well yet but I'm getting there. I owe it all to you. You gave me the courage and the ability to go that distance. I love you, Dad. I'm sorry I couldn't have gotten this done sooner." My eyes welled up with tears. I wanted so very much to have told him while he was awake and aware.

My father, of course, was unconscious so he couldn't hear what I was saying. Or could he? I'm still not sure that he could understand what I said to him. His hand which I was holding squeezed mine just a little. It could have been my imagination. I'd like to believe that it was his only way of telling me that he understood.

I looked down at him in shock. He had always been there for us. He supported us and was there for us when we needed him, but his time was drawing to a close. I put my head real close to his and I whispered. "Dad, you've done all you can for us. I know you have been in a great deal of pain. You can't do anything for us anymore. Just let it go. You deserve the rest. I'll miss you but you can't stay here any longer. All of us will get along just fine because of you." The tears streamed down my cheeks as I spoke those words.

My father passed away the next morning. I'm glad. Morning was always his favorite time of the day. He passed away quietly, without fanfare, for that is how he lived his life. His passing has left a hole in my life which I will never be able to fill. Maybe that is the way it should be. Throughout my life he filled me with all the joy and hope I could ever hope to imagine. All of that is mine to cherish and keep alive. I know that he is looking down at me at times and I think he is very proud. It took far too long but I did learn and I have taken to heart all that he tried to give me.

****

There were problems in my years with my father. Sadly, most of them were my fault. I wasn't a bad guy but I certainly caused him and my mother to have a number of sleepless nights wondering if I was ever going to get my life squared away. Eventually I did and it was directly attributable to their support and love. We argued and fought as much as any other family but we managed to get through the misunderstandings, the occasional arguments and the hurt feelings. It speaks well for both my father and my mother that they never forgot to show their love even in the midst of the problems. I don't think I have seen too many other families who can boast the same.

They didn't always listen to me; I, in turn, didn't always listen to them. Ultimately we ended up listening to each other when it really mattered. We didn't have to agree. The respectful thing to do was to listen to what the other person was thinking and saying, which we ultimately did. I know at times that was hard for my father as I had some fairly radical ideas in my youth. What stays with me are the times he cheered with me for my accomplishments, which were numerous in spite of the problems and cried with me in the bad times, never letting me feel that he was anything less than in my corner.

Through all the problems and all the accomplishments, then and now, I have known that my father loved me. If it were to mean anything to him from wherever he is now, "Dad, I remember."

Chapter 9

HEROES

What is there to say about heroes? We all have them and they are important regardless of the reason. Boys have them, men have them, girls have them, women have them. They give some meaning to our expectations and the goals toward which we reach. They may raise the level of the goals we think we would like to attain. To feel alive and to feel free I think we have to have heroes. Not all of us have perfect lives. Life sometimes is a series of troubles and problems. Heroes allow us some hope that we may persevere and overcome.

From where do our heroes come? I guess some of them come from history and some from personal experience. A hero doesn't necessarily have to be a famous figure. It might well be the woman who pulls a burning man from a building. It might be the person down the street who overcame a great adversity and managed to succeed in spite of it. Regardless from where heroes come, they should serve to inspire us to reach heights that we might ordinarily not try to attain. In my opinion they should be in some way a little mythic and personify all or some of the virtues of which all of us are capable when we put forth a little effort and a measure of courage.

When I was young, I had a number of heroes. Some came from the books I read. Of these, there were a few who were historical characters. Others, while imaginary or fictional, gave me an ideal to emulate and take as my own. From my generation forward I guess my heroes came from the screen at the movie theater and from the smaller screen of my television set. The screen was better than books because you could see what your favorite heroes did without closing your eyes. You knew what they looked like. You knew what they ate while they were out on the range or in a house. The words they spoke weren't dead and lifeless on a white page. They were dynamic and rich because they were spoken to you, in the audience, as well as to the person on the screen. The words made the character complete. The words made the ideal come to life because you heard the words. They, as mythic and heroic characters, followed what they had espoused.

God, how many times did I watch Errol Flynn defend the honor of a young woman with his blade, or sail full speed into a battle where there was no possible way to come out the winner? The heroes always won in the days when my father made his films. The heroes of the screen impacted us by portraying the very best of the ideals of human beings. It wasn't real, but then I'm not so sure that it was meant to be. It was to entertain and in some ways it was meant to educate. Ideas and morals were demonstrated before us while we watched in grand anticipation. The bad guys behaved exactly as we would have expected by being bad. The good guys, on the other hand, acted as they were supposed to have . . . by being good.

There were no gray lines to muddy the waters in those days. Heroes were allowed to have flaws in their characters. The flaws were never serious enough to make them bad guys. The bad guys may have at times been likable but when it came down to it, the bad guys behaved exactly as you would expect . . . as bad guys.

This was my father's era in the film industry. The parts he played were much in line with his own behavior. There was no doubt that he inspired a few generations of young men. So, too, did John Wayne, Errol Flynn, Jimmy Stewart, Gary Cooper and a list far too long to put on the pages of this book. I doubt that any of them took themselves all that seriously. Having met at least a few of them I know they acted very much in character to the parts they played in their films. It wasn't intentional because that was their character.

Films have changed and so have the heroes. These days we seem to want greater realism and greater technical effects.

In doing so, our heroes have become complete, with greater personal problems and more complex matters through which they must wade before they can achieve their final objective. Male or female — it doesn't really seem to matter. One thing is sure. Today's hero doesn't always look like the good guy. I know there are times when I have rooted for the bad guy, because as a person he was certainly more valuable than the good guy, who behaved more like a madman.

In the past good guys were incorruptible. In the films today it is more-or-less expected that they be corruptible. Is this the heroic image we want a new generation to view? I'm not preaching (Well, maybe I am preaching just a little.), but I think that there is a point which is worth examining. It doesn't have to be on the pages of this book but in the hearts and minds of all of us. Do you think we have gone just a bit too far in our making heroes more approachable?

I saw the cover of one of the national yellow tabloids the other day in the market. It made some statement about Bob Hope being some kind of sex fiend. Who cares? If you do care, why? Wasn't it more important that he has made a number of generations laugh? Or that he gave comfort to God only knows how many of our soldiers during World War II, the Korean War and Vietnam. I don't want to know about his personal life. If I have to bet, I bet he's just as human as I am and that would include some of the frailties and weaknesses I have and some which are exclusively his. I know he was a friend of my father's. I also know that he spent the majority of his life making people happy. At least he's still alive while they are picking on him.

I just about had heart failure when I saw the book that came out about my father and Cary Grant. Good Lord! Two men who gave us so much entertainment and company should not have to have their reputations sullied by someone who has no greater motive than to make money at the expense of their reputations. I know my father would have laughed and refused to acknowledge such accusations when he was alive. He is dead and there is no way he can defend himself. That is up to those of us who were close to him and saw him living up to the ideals which he espoused. It is recompense enough to realize that these people cannot make a reputation on their own without having to do it at someone else's expense. That is something I know my father would never have done. That makes him far better in my book.

Too, there are some books or magazines which try to belittle one of our heroes or idols. To what benefit? Does it make them more approachable? I doubt it. What it does do is confuse peoples' beliefs and aspirations. These, too, are highly suspect these days as well. To pursue the American dream and become the best you can be — whether it be in sports, movies or business — means that you are a target. You don't have to be a bad person. The fact that you are successful is enough to bear intense scrutiny, and that is pathetic.

I am well aware that I am preaching, and I am far less a conservative than my father was, but I learned well from him. I wrote this book to make a point to all those people who might have an interest in knowing that there was one man who lived up to the ideals for which he stood. There was never a moment in all the years he was alive that he acted contrary to those principals that he taught me. He was the living example of all that he spoke.

When Randolph Scott died, he had not made a picture for more than twenty four years and yet fan mail still came to the house on a weekly basis. He touched so many lives. I still get a charge when someone at a book signing comes up to me after having connected me with my father and tells me that he or she remembers my father when he or she was little. I am proud to be his son. More, I am truly grateful that I had the chance to grow up with him as not only my father, but as the man I wanted most to emulate. The sum of what I am was shaped to a great extent by the lessons I learned from my father. In being true to the ideals he taught, I have tried to live my life in a manner he would have found quite satisfying.

I thank you for allowing me to have preached and spouted throughout this book. I hope some of what I had to say was valuable to you. I know that I appreciate the fact that you bought this book. If you have read to this point, I hope I gave you what you wanted.

****

In closing this book I would like to reiterate one comment and add to it just a bit. Through all the accomplishments and all the problems then and now, I have always known that my father loved me. I saw his love and his caring throughout my whole life — not just for me but for everyone who mattered to him. If it were to mean anything to him from wherever he is, "Dad, I remember." It is not just the lessons which I remember, you see. The question that the title of this book asks: *Whatever Happened to Randolph Scott?* is answerable. I know what happened to Randolph Scott: "he is alive and well in the hearts of all whose lives he touched. Those of us who remember are richer for his having done so." He may have ridden off into the sunset to receive his final reward that I am sure was grand, but my reward was having had the opportunity to have shared so much of my life with him.

Popular press release photo

THE FILMS OF RANDOLPH SCOTT

Reprinted with permission from *Randolph Scott* by Jefferson Brim Crow, III

[1]	*Sharp Shooters*	(Fox)	1928	B/W
[2]	*The Far Call*	(Fox)	1929	B/W
[3]	*The Black Watch*	(Fox)	1929	B/W
[4]	*The Virginian*	(Paramount)	1929	B/W
[5]	*Dynamite*	(Pathe')	1929	B/W
[6]	*The Women Men Marry*	(Headline)	1931	B/W
[7]	*Sky Bride*	(Paramount)	1932	B/W
[8]	*A Successful Calamity*	(Warner Bros.)	1932	B/W
[9]	*Heritage of the Desert*	(Paramount)	1932	B/W
[10]	*Hot Saturday*	(Paramount)	1932	B/W
[11]	*Wild Horse Mesa*	(Paramount)	1932	B/W
[12]	*Hello Everybody!*	(Paramount)	1933	B/W
[13]	*The Thundering Herd*	(Paramount)	1933	B/W

Relaxing on set between scenes

[14]	*Murders in the Zoo*	(Paramount)	1933	B/W
[15]	*Supernatural*	(Paramount)	1933	B/W
[16]	*Sunset Pass*	(Paramount)	1933	B/W
[17]	*Cocktail Hour*	(Columbia)	1933	B/W
[18]	*Man of the Forest*	(Paramount)	1933	B/W
[19]	*To the Last Man*	(Paramount)	1933	B/W
[20]	*Broken Dreams*	(Monogram)	1934	B/W
[21]	*The Last Roundup*	(Paramount)	1934	B/W
[22]	*Wagon Wheels*	(Paramount)	1934	B/W
[23]	*Home on the Range*	(Paramount)	1935	B/W
[24]	*Rocky Mountain Mystery*	(Paramount)	1935	B/W
[25]	*Roberta*	(RKO)	1935	B/W
[26]	*Village Tale*	(RKO)	1935	B/W
[27]	*She*	(RKO)	1935	B/W
[28]	*So Red the Rose*	(Paramount)	1935	B/W
[29]	*Follow the Fleet*	(RKO-Radio)	1936	B/W
[30]	*And Sudden Death*	(Paramount)	1936	B/W
[31]	*The Last of the Mohicans*	(United Artists)	1936	B/W
[32]	*Go West Young Man*	(Paramount)	1936	B/W
[33]	*High Wide and Handsome*	(Paramount)	1937	B/W
[34]	*Rebecca of Sunnybrook Farm*	(Fox)	1938	B/W
[35]	*The Road to Reno*	(Universal)	1938	B/W

Scene from BADMAN'S TERRITORY

[36]	*The Texans*	(Paramount)	1938	B/W
[37]	*Jesse James*	(Fox)	1939	Technicolor
[38]	*Susanna of the Mounties*	(Fox)	1939	Sepiatone
[39]	*Frontier Marshal*	(Fox)	1939	B/W
[40]	*Coast Guard*	(Columbia)	1939	B/W
[41]	*20,000 Men a Year*	(Fox)	1939	B/W
[42]	*Virginia City*	(Warner Bros.)	1940	B/W
[43]	*My Favorite Wife*	(RKO-Radio)	1940	B/W
[44]	*When the Daltons Rode*	(Universal)	1940	B/W
[45]	*Western Union*	(Fox)	1941	B/W
[46]	*Belle Starr*	(Fox)	1941	B/W
[47]	*Paris Calling*	(Universal)	1941	B/W
[48]	*To the Shores of Tripoli*	(Fox)	1942	Technicolor
[49]	*The Spoilers*	(Universal)	1942	B/W
[50]	*Pittsburgh*	(Universal)	1942	B/W
[51]	*The Desperadoes*	(Columbia)	1943	Technicolor
[52]	*Bombardier*	(RKO)	1943	B/W
[53]	*Corvette K-225*	(Universal)	1943	B/W
[54]	*Gung Ho!*	(Universal)	1943	B/W
[55]	*Follow the Boys*	(Universal)	1944	B/W
[56]	*Belle of the Yukon*	(RKO)	1944	B/W
[57]	*China Sky*	(RKO)	1945	B/W

. . . with Phyllis Thaxter in a scene from FORT WORTH

[58] *Captain Kidd*   (United Artists) 1945   B/W

[59] *Abilene Town*   (United Artists) 1946   B/W

[60] *Badman's Territory*   (RKO)   1946   B/W

[61] *Home, Sweet Homicide*   (Fox)   1946   B/W

[62] *Trail Street*   (RKO-Radio)   1947   B/W

[63] *Gunfighters*   (Columbia)   1947   Cinecolor

[64] *Christmas Eve*   (United Artists) 1947   B/W

[65] *Albuquerque*   (Paramount)   1948   Cinecolor

[66] *Coroner Creek*   (Columbia)   1948   Cinecolor

[67] *Return of the Badmen*   (RKO)   1948   B/W

[68] *Canadian Pacific*   (Fox)   1949   Color

[69] *The Walking Hills*   (Columbia)   1949   B/W

[70] *The Doolins of Oklahoma*   (Columbia)   1949   B/W

[71] *Fighting Man of the Plains*   (Fox)   1949   Cinecolor

[72] *The Nevadan*   (Columbia)   1950   Cinecolor

[73] *Colt .45*   (Warner Bros.)   1950   Technicolor

[74] *The Cariboo Trail*   (Fox)   1950   Cinecolor

[75] *Sugarfoot*   (Warner Bros.)   1951   Technicolor

[76] *Starlift*   (Warner Bros.)   1951   Color

[77] *Santa Fe*   (Columbia)   1951   Technicolor

[78] *Fort Worth*   (Warmer Bros.)   1951   Technicolor

[79] *Man in the Saddle*   (Columbia)   1951   Technicolor

Publicity still to promote TALL MAN RIDING

[80]	*Carson City*	(Warner Bros.)	1952	WarnerColor
[81]	*Hangman's Knot*	(Columbia)	1952	Technicolor
[82]	*The Man Behind the Gun*	(Warner Bros.)	1953	Technicolor
[83]	*The Stranger Wore a Gun*	(Columbia)	1953	Technicolor 3-D
[84]	*Thunder Over the Plains*	(Warner Bros.)	1953	Warnercolor
[85]	*Riding Shotgun*	(Warner Bros.)	1954	WarnerColor
[86]	*The Bounty Hunter*	(Transconal/ Warner Bros.)	1954	WarnerColor
[87]	*Ten Wanted Men*	(Columbia)	1955	Technicolor
[88]	*Rage at Dawn*	(RKO)	1955	Technicolor
[89]	*Tall Man Riding*	(Warner Bros.)	1955	WarnerColor
[90]	*A Lawless Street*	(Columbia)	1955	Technicolor
[91]	*Seven Men From Now*	(Warner Bros.)	1956	WarnerColor
[92]	*7th Cavalry*	(Columbia)	1956	Technicolor
[93]	*The Tall T*	(Columbia)	1957	Technicolor
[94]	*Shoot-out at Medicine Bend*	(Warner Bros.)	1957	B/W
[95]	*Decision at Sundown*	(Columbia)	1957	Technicolor
[96]	*Buchanan Rides Alone*	(Columbia)	1958	Technicolor
[97]	*Ride Lonesome*	(Columbia)	1959	Eastman Color
[98]	*Westbound*	(Warner Bros.)	1959	WarnerColor
[99]	*Comanche Station*	(Columbia)	1960	Eastman Color
[100]	*Ride the High Country*	(MGM)	1962	Metrocolor